THE WAY OF THE BUFFALO

A Business Primer
& Fashion Love Song

SPENCER BLOCK

Kestni Bloch

ISBN 978-0-615-43069-1

Cover Design by Joe Pagac

Set in Palatino Linotype, and Dom Casual

"Spencer Block: Scant Fashion Sense, Tons of Business
Savvy" written by Kimberly Matas has been reprinted with
permission from Arizona Daily Star

Awards Plaque art © 2011 Janet K. Miller

For Spencer Barry Block
March 27, 1940 - September 6, 2009

"First Spencer showed me how to live and then he
showed me how to die"
—Michael March

Foreword and Acknowledgments

It was Spencer's goal to write this book. As time passed it became obvious that he would not be able to finish it before he died. First he saw it as a continuous, logical textbook; then he simplified his vision to a collection of essays. We have assembled his writings, speeches, and lectures in this book, in a somewhat topical fashion. Since he wrote and rewrote prolifically, we sorted through his continuously refined work and tried to ferret out what he considered his final word on a particular subject.

Our thanks to the unusual and extraordinary individuals who contributed to the philosophy of Buffalo Exchange: Tito Haggardt, our loyal, smart, and insightful friend, who showed us early on that growing our company culture was an essential ingredient to our business. Mark Weiss, PhD, guru, business consultant, and friend, who taught us the Five Points of Power and how to hold ourselves and others responsible for our own and their actions. Jack Stack, the originator of the Great Game of Business®, who showed us the way to open-book management.

This project could not have been completed without the commitment of Inara Edrington, Buffalo Exchange archivist and researcher extraordinaire, and Milani Hunt, Buffalo Exchange ex-marketing director, who took on the daunting task of organizing Spencer's many writings into book format.

We think we have come up with a book that Spencer would have approved of. We feel it portrays what he believed in and communicates the uniqueness of his person. Our wish is that it keeps his perspective and personality alive for us and for Buffalo Exchange. In this book Spencer shows us how to live and work the Buffalo Way.

—Kerstin and Rebecca Block

Dedication

To all the people who have worked with Buffalo Exchange over all the years—the good, the bad, but never the ugly. They have all been beautiful, whether helping to build the company and themselves or stealing from us. Here's to them all. They wove the intricate and beautiful textile that we became. The wings that made it possible to fly.

This book is dedicated to all our fellow business folks and to those in our families who came before us and taught us the basics of being human while being in business. To all of us who know what it is to struggle to earn enough to take care of ourselves and our families while still being our own bosses.

The Way of the Buffalo is about the spirit of the entrepreneur. The will to sell, the joy and the art of providing products and services to the public. The ways of organizing and weaving through the maze of life, of people, of governments, the law, and not least, your own way of being.

This is a spiritual journey, not a handbook on how to do it, but rather lessons learned by two small-time entrepreneurs over a three-decade experience of the business of business.

—Spencer Block

Company Meeting, 2009

CONTENTS

Preface

This book is a distillation of 30-plus years of business experience. It's a patchwork of history and lessons learned. Its aim is to help people be successful in business and hopefully in their lives. It offers no fast track way to the top but rather the "Way of the Buffalo"—steady and rewarding at every stage.

Like in any historical or biographical enterprise, the good will be emphasized and the bad will be played down. However, hopefully a truth will emerge in spite of these distortions, and the path that we have followed will emerge clearly.

Buffaloes don't like to fly. They have their own way of getting around; and to be a buffalo, one has to learn how to do this—how to adapt to the path—how to become one through and through. This may mean getting there more slowly but intact, with integrity. After 30 years of learning from the buffalo, we thought we might put down what we think we know in this small volume.

Thirty years ago we hopped on the back of a buffalo with wings and took off for a flight of fancy, adventure, and fun.

We are still flying. What we learned along the way, we have tried to pass on through mentoring, workshops, and limited writings.

At some point, we decided that we should write a little history pamphlet for our progeny and anyone else who had an interest in our experience. As we added more, we became aware that we had a lot more material to put down. The results are this book.

Buffalo Lore

The first Buffalo Exchange opened January 15, 1974, in Tucson, Arizona, by Kerstin and Spencer Block. To their knowledge, this was the very first store that bought, sold, traded, and took clothing items and accessories on consignment.

Kerstin Block, the mother of two, had been fired from her job as a decorator for a furniture retailer and had tried to learn secretarial skills at the local community college and failed. Spencer had landed a job at the University of Arizona in Tucson. With at least one income source secured, Kerstin decided to follow her passion and open a used clothing store near the University campus.

The name of her venture resulted from a combination of factors. Since the store concept deals with both consignment and paying cash for clothing, a decision was reached to call it an "exchange." Kerstin, a Swedish immigrant, picked the word "buffalo" because the word conjured up Western Americana. The name "Buffalo Exchange" was born.

Kerstin's days were filled with being the mother of two young school-aged girls, thrift shopping for clothing to put in the shop, and running the shop, including taking clothing in on consignment or buying outright from the public.

Spencer came in periodically to help run the register and do incidental repair and maintenance handiwork. He hung the bicycle wheels from the ceiling and assembled the water pipes for racks, put up the shelves, etc.

After six months, Spencer quit his job at the University of Arizona and devoted all his time to the store, which was beginning to earn a living for the family. Spencer remembered their first $1,000.00 day, a Saturday. "We couldn't believe it! It was like a dream. Actually, we had trouble digesting our first sale, which we remember as an old leather vest of mine. Somebody actually spent money in our store."

Why? Why did it work so well right off the bat? Their guess: Kerstin and Spencer were good at what they were doing.

Kerstin had a fantastic sense of fashion and marketing. The store was completely charming and the inventory was well-priced and desirable. She knew what would sell to her fashion-conscious clientele, and that clientele responded with resounding support.

Spencer understood how to organize the support structure of the operation—bookkeeping, insurance, physical plant, advertising, etc. He also knew how to stay out of the way of the artistic end of the operation and let Kerstin forge her own reality. He ran the register, tagged, hung clothing, made sure customers were acknowledged and taken care of, developed systems for handling consignments, did all the paperwork, and then joyfully counted the cash at the end of each day.

The daughters could walk from their school to the store. After school, they would come and help out doing simple tasks. There was an old black-and-white TV that was kept in the back, which they could watch after they finished their tasks.

At the end of the day, they closed up and went home. But the excitement of the day—the gratification of knowing that they were in the right place doing what they were good at—stayed with them and gave them a nice feeling of well-being. The next day was always seen with great anticipation as if a great reward was to be bestowed. And it was.

For years we thought our success in this period was due in great part to the time and place, and that we had just been lucky. Probably the timing helped a bit; what we have learned over the last three and one-half decades is that timing is a small issue for our business. Fashion goes on and on. As far as location goes, it is important; but Kerstin had the intuition to understand that. It was not luck.

It was the right people doing the right things. If this sounds smug, it is not meant to be. It is just that there are so many people who start businesses without the right combination of love and skills and then blame their failures on luck. Luck is not a critical element of success in small business.

The Way of the Buffalo is for entrepreneurs—risk takers. It is not for everyone. There are some whose nature craves security and stability. This is not the path that we describe here. Rather, this is the way of innovation, creativity, and openness to the world that surrounds and teaches us.

Always listen to the trees. If you can hear the trees, you will hear all the other elements that will help you to steer your course.

Kerstin and Spencer Block, ca. 1975

Chapter 1
The
Essence Of Business

REAL MONEY

That's what we pay for clothes. Also we trade BUT — what is most important is that we sell what we buy; and since we only pay real money for the best, that's what we sell!

THE BEST IN NEW
AND RECYCLED CLOTHING

BUFFALO
EXCHANGE

The Zen of the Buffalo

The sayings of Master Chip:

"If you do not love your buffalo, she will not be happy and thus will not give as much milk; nor will she pull the wagon willingly. She will step on your children out of depression or carelessness and even though she will continue to love you, she will be restless and ill at ease around you. At night, she may bellow so loudly that your neighbors will come and throw rocks at your house, and all the world will know that here lives an unloved buffalo."

Lesson Number One: Forget Reality

The North American bison, better known as the buffalo, did not fly. If it could have, it might have survived in great numbers. Instead it was decimated, the remainder relegated to reservations.

This is our legacy. We have had to learn to fly or become extinct—succeed or die like so many other businesses before us. The trick, of course, is how to learn to fly.

Lesson number one: Forget Reality.

Reality has no place in flying. Reality tells you that a big metal machine or a buffalo cannot stay up in the air. This has to be forgotten and a new mentality has to take its place. The vision of a buffalo with wings in the air has to become the new reality.

Going To Work

I've had people tell me that going to work was like giving up part of their life. How sad. Work should be a joy, something to look forward to. When you are on your deathbed, you should be able to say, "I don't regret one minute spent at work. Those were some of the best minutes of my life." Your work is your life. It is an extension of your existence. For those who think they are in the wrong job, remember the song lyrics: "If you can't be with the one you love, love the one you're with." Always bless your work.

Spencer Block, ca. 1975

Johny Mac

My father taught me that there was no job that I was too good to do, that all work is holy, that to do work is a blessing and to do work that you love is a double blessing.

When I was 11, my father decided that I should go to work in one of our fish stores. We had five of them at the time. They were in black neighborhoods on the South Side of Chicago. He drove me over to the one on 43rd Street one summer day and handed me over to Johny Mac Clayton, the store manager.

Johny Mac was a tough-looking black man, the kind you cross the street to avoid if possible, because his face looked like it was on the verge of being mad. His shiny black arms were big and rounded out with muscles that needed no flexing to show through his white t-shirt. He didn't smile much. He didn't seem to like me or my dad.

"Treat him like any other worker," my dad said. It was what I expected him to say. "You know how to get home on the 'L'?"

"Yeah" and then Dad was gone.

"First you need to dress," Johny Mac said as he looked down at me with a slightly warm touch of a smile, handing me a fresh, white, starched apron. "Then we get to work." He handed me a flashlight. "Cats keep the place clean of rats and mice. You need to keep the cats' house clean."

Customers

The lifeblood of our business is our customers. When we talk of customer relations or customer service, we are talking about service. The most important people we deal with—our partners in the game—are our customers.

When I worked in the store in the early days, I went nuts over customers. I loved them.

They brought me money. They fed me. They came into the store and brought me things to sell. They kept me entertained. They talked to me and smiled, and I felt good.

They were bright lights. They were smart, kind, beautiful souls that made me happy to get up in the morning and go to meet them in the store. They made good days out of bad ones. They were my friends and my talk-mates.

Over the years, I saw their children grow, their relatives and friends die, and their lives change forever. And still they came to seek the small pleasures of the world of vision, of dressing and looking good. Most were women, but many were men. All ages. All sizes. All kinds.

The word "customer" is too cold to describe what these people were—and still are—to me.

I feel sorry for anyone who lives in the world of retail and doesn't love these people.

It must be very sad for them, very hard, very difficult.

Kerstin and Ruth Williams (customer)

Some Basic Beliefs and Values of Buffalo Exchange

Every business has to have something at its core that dictates how it operates: the philosophical and moral rules of the game.

1. A business should always strive to make money without exploitation of people, the environment, or the eco-systems of the world.

2. Living things, besides humans, are important and essential to the quality of life. These plants and animals must be respected, valued, and protected where necessary.

3. Reusing and recycling resources is an important way of helping to preserve the environment and the biodiversity that is essential to the well-being of the planet.

4. Individuals are primarily responsible for their decisions and actions or lack of action. To the extent that we do not allow individuals to experience the consequences of their actions, we foster dependence and a lack of self-confidence, and show a great disrespect for them.

5. A society should aid those who are victims, those who, through no fault of their own, are in circumstances of desperation.

6. Buffalo Exchange is a learning organization. We can only continue to exist if we continue to learn.

7. People are what Buffalo Exchange is. We are nothing more or less than the people involved in our enterprise, the employees and the customers.

8. The golden rule applies in both its forms:

    • Rabbi Hillel's version: "Do unto others what you would not have done unto you."

    • The good old version: "Do unto others as you would have them do unto you."

9. Work should be an exciting, enjoyable, enriching experience of self-actualization.

10. Each individual is worthy of respect and is to be treated with dignity, unless and until (s)he forfeits that right by certain behavior.

Cash Register: The Musical

I've stood behind here
For a thousand years
It seems
I've stood and wished away
A thousand dreams
It seems
I've offered "Can I help you"
At least a hundred thousand times

And I've heard the sound of money
In the corners of my mind

Cash register
It's where life has found its force

Cash register
It's the money of course

I have stood here for a thousand years
It seems

My days have tumbled by
In cascades of muffled screams

As I traded goods
And gave my life
To put food on the table
I came each day and went
each night
And found that I was able

To cross that holy threshold
And see that holy light
I got a life of food and shelter
And a place instead of a fight

Beyond Your Comfort Zone

Think like a seller or a customer. Don't think like a store-keeper. Arrange for your customers, not for yourself. If you set it up for your convenience, you'll convenience yourself out of business.

The current reality: People are time-stressed. They don't have time, especially the ones with good clothes and money. Work with that. Competition has changed. Discount dealers have reduced costs of clothing. You must act accordingly. Businesses have gone casual. People have lots of other places to spend money now—catalog shopping, items other than clothing. Catalogs offer 24-hour ordering and 24-hour shipping. TV shopping, and on-line shopping. If you can save your customer time, you will be a winner. Make shopping easy.

What customers want: To be considered. Uniqueness, convenience, variety, consistency, ease of shopping.

Under promise, and over deliver.

In your personal life, work for effectiveness, not efficiency.

Change should be easier for resellers than for dealers in new items. We can change faster. We should take advantage of this. Welcome change as an adventure that can lead to delight.

Ask your customers what they want. Ask customers to take surveys. Bribe customers to participate with some sort of discount coupon or whatever. Give them something for their trouble.

We need to keep actively thinking about what we are doing and not settle into what we perceive to be a comfort zone, because that comfort zone may turn out to be the danger zone.

In Honor of Ira

The end of a year, the end of a life. Ira, our female cat of 19 years, was put to sleep December 19th, 1990.

She was there at the beginning of Buffalo Exchange and saw us through all of our growing years in the business as well as in our personal lives.

She saw us through goat breeding, dairy farming, chickens, gerbils, dogs, other cats, and a host of unmentionable things.

She taught us many things not the least of which was that things change, things die, things are born, and that all of this is essential.

At the beginning of the New Year, we will spread her ashes around the acreage surrounding our house where she ranged and got serious about lizards, quail, and small critters.

Kerstin and Ira, ca. 1978

Chapter 2
The Golden Rules
of Business

The Five Points of Power

Every so often, when the rare occasion arises and someone asks me about Buffalo Exchange, one of the most common questions is, "How do you manage to have so many stores with so many people in so many places?" I generally tell them that I don't know. That cuts the conversation short, takes me off the hook, and keeps me from seeming like a fool, which I might were I to give them the real answer.

The fact is that I do know. But the truth is so simple that it almost sounds dumb. So I keep it a big secret. However, in the spirit of openness, I shall give you the single word answer: trust.

In order to turn a person loose a few hundred or a few thousand miles away to run a shop, manage people, manage a physical plant, manage an inventory, spend huge amounts of the company's money, be in a position to cost the company huge amounts of money, etc., in order to do this, there has to be a level of trust between the company and the individual— in this case, the store manager. I have found that there are five ways to build trust. Doing each of these increases the level of trust. Not doing these destroys it.

The tricky thing about trust is that it is a very fragile thing that exists in the air and in the minds and hearts of people. It is fragile because it takes a lot of effort to create and very little effort to destroy. It has been described as a bank account that builds slowly with many small deposits, but can be wiped out with one big withdrawal.

So where does this bring us? How does this apply to you? Maybe it doesn't. But, let me recount some historical information you might find interesting. Except for incompetence, the major reasons for management personnel separating from the company have had to do with trust. Buffalo Exchange has worked diligently to build trust between itself and its employees. One of the inspirations for open-book management has been the trust factor. It's a way of "speaking the truth" to all employees.

One aspect of the Career Track (the Employee Development Plan) program was that it offered consistency and reliability — two features of "keeping agreements." In short, we try hard to live up to our own philosophy of doing business; and, by the same token, we demand that same level of behavior from those who work with us. Without trust, we would just be another poorly managed business with a short life span.

Speak the Truth

Not for others, but for yourself. It feels clean. It is a quick path to self-respect. Every lie, every hidden act, eats away at your vision of what you are.

Always level with your customers. We decided to tell them exactly what we would sell their items for and what their percentage would be. Later, we learned to level with the employees by having open-book management, which we learned from The Great Game of Business® people. Watch your words. Pick short simple ones that are more powerful. Don't give away your power. You need it.

Training an employee requires simple words said consistently. Be direct and succinct. Don't beat around the bush. You will be surprised how it will not kill you.

Keep Your Agreements

Especially with employees. We expect them to keep theirs, and we keep ours. Ninety percent of problems we have with employees can be traced back to a lack of someone keeping an agreement. Never promise what you cannot deliver. Be very careful about making commitments. It's better to say "no" or "I will think about it" than to change your mind later or just not perform.

Do not use *give away power* or *promising* phrases such as: "I will check with my area manager" or "I am sure we can do that, but let me check." Once you give your word, you are stuck. Since you speak for the company, the company is also stuck. Always be consistent and reliable. That is an agreement built into your job. Always follow through. That is another agreement that is built into your job. Once you say it, do it.

Take Responsibility for Your Decision and Actions

When I hire, one of the threads I look for on the application and in the interview is whether or not this person takes responsibility for his or her life. Reviewing why they left previous jobs or want to leave the one they have are good indicators.

"Disagreement with manager" or "personal reasons" are good indicators of problems in this area.

Bad-mouthing previous employers is another indicator of a responsibility deficit. Listening carefully to their tone and words can give you all the clues you need. Are they victims or are they people who take control of situations in their lives and make things work for them? Pick the latter. Victims don't do well in the world of work. They make managing miserable.

What about you? Are you a victim of the construction down the street that has cut your foot traffic? Do you firmly believe that the drop in sales is because your floor has not been re-done yet? Do you blame the economy?

The funny thing about taking responsibility is that if you do not, you cannot grow. If everything is someone else's fault or the fault of great outside forces, then you are perfect and have no need to improve. What a nice place to be. What little effort that takes. How fast you will be gone. We, Buffalo Exchange, need people to manage who are continuously better. It's the shark scenario. Sharks cannot get enough oxygen unless they are moving. Need I spell out that analogy?

When stuff goes wrong in this company, I assume that it's my fault. The euphemism I use is that effluent flows downhill. Bad stuff starts at the top. If you are managing poorly, it is because I am allowing it to happen. I am not pushing Kerstin and Rebecca to push the Chief Operations Officer to push the Area Manager to push you or get rid of you. But it's my fault. The buck stops here. That reportedly was a sign on Harry Truman's desk. Harry Truman, you may remember, was the President who authorized dropping bombs on Hiroshima and Nagasaki. What a burden to bear.

What guts to take it all and say, "It was my decision; right or wrong, it was mine." That's taking responsibility.

When sales are down at your store, what will you say? What will you honestly feel about it? If you look to yourself first, you will have a chance at success. If your hands go up in a pointing motion towards somebody or something else, you will be on the road to stagnation and failure.

I have talked so far about being tough. Now I am going to talk about being cued in—not soft or easy, but sensitive and alert to the needs and behaviors of others. I am going to talk about stepping outside of yourself and imagining things— imagining what the other person is feeling and thinking.

This is not mystical: it is just a way of thinking about how to focus on others.

Give 100% Attention

When you deal with people, give them all of your attention. Be strong, be there. This is obvious. If you are talking to someone and then break it off for your ringing phone, what are you telling the person you are talking to? If you talk to someone and keep looking at the sales floor to see how things are going, what is the message? One hundred percent attention is an essential ingredient in any successful human interaction. Without it, you are showing disrespect and can not fully interact. It's obvious. But it is rare that we give it.

Here are a couple of tips:

- **Location**: Make sure it is quiet and free from distractions.

- **Positioning**: Face the person. If possible, try not to have big desk or table keeping you apart.

- **Make eye contact**: In some cultures, this is considered a challenging posture, but we are stuck with our culture; thus try to be sensitive about this.

- **Listen**: Active listening is a very effective technique. Learn how to use it. In its simplest form it is a two-way communication method whereby you are continuously confirming that you have heard the person and that you have heard the person correctly.

I was once chair of the board for a local food coop. The board was so fiercely divided on various issues that board meetings often turned into verbal fights that stalled the entire process. In desperation, I instigated a rule that no one could speak in the open forum discussions until he or she restated what the last person had said to that person's satisfaction. It was an amazing experience.

At the beginning, most people couldn't even get close to restating even the basics of what the previous speaker had said until the fourth or fifth try. The distortions in what they thought they had heard were extraordinary. For example, a speaker might say something totally innocuous about a financial statement item; and the next speaker who was reacting would interpret it as a personal attack and would be incapable of restating what had been said seconds earlier without distortions and added negative verbiage.

As we went on with this exercise, board members became much better at listening to each other, since they realized that they would not get to speak until they got it right. When you listen, get it right. Don't add. Listen between the lines, but don't get that mixed up with what the person has actually said. Summarize what is being said back to the person, and always try to get to "yes, that's it."

Ask For What You Want

Ask for what you want and need. If you don't say it out loud, it won't go anywhere. Be clear. Be succinct. Do it politely, but directly. Don't mince your words. Don't be vague. People can't read your mind.

These are the Five Points of Power:

1. Speak the truth.

2. Keep your agreements.

3. Take responsibility for your decisions and actions.

4. Give 100% attention.

5. Ask for what you want.

These are simple, and to the extent that they are simple, they are hard to do. But as you get better at them, you will realize that they will not kill you and will make you stronger. They will make your job much easier. They will change your life. They will help you manage to survive.

Mark Weiss

It's Up To You

Basically it all boils down to trying to be good, and that requires that you define good. That is an issue that mankind (humans, if you will) has been grappling with since the beginning of conscience.

There is one principle that I would like to stress, because I believe that in this time of American cultural evolution it is being blurred.

"Take responsibility for your actions" is what it says in the Five Points of Power. I say, "Be accountable for your own experience. "

In essence, this is an issue of fairness. Is it fair for me to carry you, because you made stupid decisions and did some dumb things? How far should I carry you? If I do, I am not being fair to the other employees that make a living from working with this company.

It's not the economy, it's not the competition, it's not the lack of an office building or the lack of air-conditioning. It's you. And it's up to you to make it work. That's what Buffalo Exchange is all about.

Learn about The Great Game of Business®. If you take three main concepts away with you, this book will be considered a successful project that was worth the cost to the company.

First: And most important is the idea that IT'S UP TO YOU.

There are no victims in this organization. There are no excuses. It's the joy of making it. If there is no chance of failure, there's no joy of success. This means you accept full responsibility for what you decide, what you do, and what you do not do. It's not the economy.

Second: Business is a lot like a game, it has rules, it involves risk, and you KEEP SCORE. Keeping score—knowing where we are in the game.

Third: The one rule that we can never forget about our business is that we make money—that we STAY ALIVE—BY SELLING.

A corollary to this basic fact is that everything we do has to be done with that aim in mind. If it's not helping us to sell, why are we doing it?

Let me repeat the first concept: IT'S UP TO YOU. Therefore IT'S UP TO YOU to make it work. That's what Buffalo Exchange is all about. IT'S UP TO YOU means that you accept full responsibility for what you decide you do, and what you do not do. It means you can never be a victim of circumstances. Excuses are not allowed. Performance is what counts. It means that somebody believes in you and your ability to make it happen. It means that you are given the opportunity to be all that you can—to self-actualize.

Is it fair? We think it is. Is it practical? It is our belief that without an organization of people who are ready, willing, and able to take on this kind of responsibility, our survival is not possible.

Does this mean we will not support and encourage you? Of course not.

It simply means that YOU are the one who does the doing. We can only do so much. If you are willing to take this challenge—to seize the opportunity to learn business and be in business, Buffalo Exchange needs you. A company that wants to last 100 years has to find, engage, and nurture such people for its continued well-being.

Also important are the personal philosophies of each individual. During a company meeting I asked the employees to break up into six groups.

Each group was asked to contribute its own group philosophy in a single sentence. The contributions were:

1. Life is too short not to be the best person you can be.

2. You get what you give.

3. The possibilities are limitless.

4. Know yourself. Know your power. Take action. Care.

5. Symbiotic respect and enrichment.

6. In all things there is the potential for goodness. It's up to you.

Canoe Pickett, Spencer & Kerstin Block, 1994

Manager Rap

Remember Harry Truman?
When he heard a lotta bitchin'
Said "If you can't take the heat,
Get out of the kitchen"

He was my kind of manager
Not a lot to fear
Had a sign on his desk
Said "The buck stops here"

So I'll do some repeating
In case you didn't get
my meaning

It you can't take the heat
Get out of the kitchen
It's in your hands
So stop your bitchin'

You got goals to make
You got people to move
You gotta learn to survive
So get in the groove

The finger pointin' game
Is all bad news
All it's gonna get you
Is the stagnation blues

The saddest thing
I've ever been told
Is "It's not my fault
about the cost of
goods sold"

You gotta understand
It's your psychology
Not the economy
Or geography
Or not even the sociology

The ball's in your court
Now it's your play
The finger pointin' game
Is for yesterday

So buckle up buckaroos
Hear the good news
It's a new day a comin'
But it's all up to you

Drugs in the Workplace

We used to joke that our drug testing program was simple: you bring us the drugs and we'll test them. Although a rather flippant approach to a very real problem, upon careful examination, it turns out that that approach probably makes about as much sense as what some companies do.

After years of periodically considering a drug testing program, we decided that the amount of damage that would be done by instituting such a program would be far greater than the benefit we might gain, if any. Our company is based on our people—those who work for us. Now, as I write this, there are more than 500 people working in the Buffalo Exchange enterprise. These folks do what they do for a lot of different reasons; but two major factors that bind them to the company are that they are treated with respect and they are trusted. It makes no difference whether or not each and every one of them deserves to be trusted. It is, of course, a fact that that is not the case. But they are trusted to act honorably, and the great majority of them do so willingly, happily, and enthusiastically. When they see fellow employees not acting in a trustworthy manner, most of the time, they do something about it by either trying to influence the trust-breaker or by reporting it. Over the years, the most common way we have discovered cheating on the part of employees is from information given to us by other employees who have found the actions of the cheaters to be unfair and distasteful.

This is the kind of morale and commitment that drug testing would chip away. This is the kind of connection and union that a company should have with its employees. Is it an ideal that is unattainable? Is it a method of exploitation, a way of trying to get the most effort for the least amount of pay? I imagine that if that is the strategy, then it could be construed so. The Buffalo Way is to continually work toward fairness, toward a situation in which all those engaged in the effort are rewarded in an equitable manner.

It is not a democracy we have worked toward creating, but rather a flexible entity that strives to do what is right for all those involved.

To do so, it has to listen, to continuously review its policies and procedures, and to refuse to accept that it has the inside knowledge of what is true. It is the stance of the tentative beginner. It is the stance of the learner.

So, do we have people in the company doing drugs? Yes. Should they be working for Buffalo Exchange? Probably not. Should we weed them out? In this environment, they will weed themselves out. They will fail to perform adequately or they will turn to some sort of scheme to cheat the company in order to support their drug habit. Either way, they will end up gone. Or, in some rare cases, they will be able to do the job and operate within the framework of trust and fairness. In that case, they are where they should be, and are part of what we are.

Spencer, ca. 1980

Ask the Question

A newlywed was confronted with cooking her very first fresh ham.

Not knowing quite what to do, she phoned her mother who instructed her to first set the ham out in front of her with the small end to the right.

Then she was to cut off three to five inches of the small end, and then season the ham, etc., and cook it for a certain amount of time.

However, she became curious as to why it was important to cut off part of the small end of the ham?

So, she called her mother and asked. Her mother wasn't sure. It seemed that was how her mother had always done it. So she called her grandmother and inquired why she had always cut off the small end of the ham.

"Well," her grandmother answered, "I didn't have a big enough pan to cook it in."

I know that some of what we do in business day-in-and-day-out is equivalent to cutting off part of the small end of the ham.

And if it works, why fix it? Why? Because you can waste a lot of ham over the years for absolutely no good reason. Not only that, but as competition increases, that ham may be your profit.

Honor Your Goose

March 2006

First, we have finally evolved into something different from all the rest of the pack. We have become fashion; and we have to be careful to remain humble about it. We are the place where people who love clothing come, not just to get stuff, but to see us—what we are wearing—and to hear us—what we are saying about style and who knows what else. They also come to see and be with other customers who populate our stores—to see what they are wearing and doing, and saying. It's no accident that we are in cool places all over the country and will continue to move in that direction. We have found our passion and have managed to stamp that image on ourselves and the public. This is not true of all our stores yet; but it is becoming the truth. Being conscious of it is powerful and dangerous at the same time. I'll let you dwell on that one.

Those of us who are not into this enthrallment but are dedicated to the company and its success have to deal with this reality—this company persona—without allowing ourselves to become alienated in the process. My advice is simple: respect it and honor it. It is, after all, the Golden Goose. Our job is to support, nurture, and protect it. It is what feeds us all.

My First Landlord

Buffalo Exchange 1974

My first landlord was an older fellow who had been in business a long time. He had good business sense. He rented us our little 400 square foot space, and after around six months or so, he allowed us to rent the space next store. Now we had 800 square feet. We paid our rent on time. Always.

After a year, the time came to renew our lease. I was nervous about any steep increase in rent. We had been doing well, but a big increase could cut down our profits severely and possibly limit the profits to a point where it would not be worth continuing.

I met with the old man. "You're doing well, it looks like," he started out.

"Yes," I reluctantly admitted, thinking this was his beginning salvo into a tough negotiation to squeeze out of us all he could get.

"You're a good tenant," he said next. I figured this was the compliment before the bad news. "You pay on time. You keep the place nice," he went on. "You got a nice business going here, but you got to make a living. You know the rent should go up. You tell me what you think you should pay."
I had an idea of what I thought a fair increase would be, and I told him.

"That sounds ok," he said after a little hesitation. And we shook hands.

I learned something from that old man—something that became a part of the Buffalo Way: The goose that lays the golden eggs doesn't have to lay big eggs, it just has to keep on laying.

Goal Setting

As you know, goal setting is not a science. I think about it. I remember the old adage about democracy which, to paraphrase, says that democracy is a terrible form of government but the best one that we have found so far.

In order to truly delegate responsibility for store operations to Area Managers and to Store Managers, we had to devise a system of controls and accountability (eg. Dale Carnegie Training©). This method of management requires that individuals be given information on where we want them to go and not a specific set of instructions on how to get there. To elaborate, many organizations tell people exactly what to do in every single circumstance that might arise. Our method is to tell people where we want them to get to and allow them to make decisions on how to do it—how to get there.

In order to do the above, however, goals of some sort have to be articulated. The goals are where we want things to go. Without goals we will never know if we get there or not. And above all, the goal setting should be an interactive activity with managers and area managers having input.

Once the goals are set, there they are. To change them after the fact is to negate them, unless it's obvious that major factors were not considered.

The important thing to remember about goal setting is that it does have some basis in logic. It is either a comparison with previous years or previous stores or something else previous. It usually has some historical basis. Often we will use figures from the previous year and make adjustments according to various factors. With new stores we will often rely on data gathered from other new stores—sales per square foot, etc.

Why Is My Business Failing?

1. Because your ego got in the way.
2. Because you did not watch and/or believe the numbers.
3. Because your plan had a serious flaw.

Ego: You thought you had the greatest thing, idea, product, whatever that mankind needed. You did not pay attention to what anyone told you about how it might not be all that great. Your sources—friends, associates, etc.—were polite for the most part, not wanting to alienate such an enthusiastic and passionate person. The subtle clues they gave you about the project's possible problems passed you by. You were too much involved. You should have been able to step outside yourself and see it from their perspective. Your ego prevented this. You lose.

Believe the numbers: A business that shows a loss is not making it. Face up to it. The sooner the better. If you find yourself rationalizing away bad numbers, you are rationalizing away your bank account. Try burning a couple of $100 bills to make the experience a little less theoretical.

Flawed Plan: Even if you did not have a plan, you actually did have a plan: it simply was not articulated as such. This often happens when the plan is so stupid that one does not want to articulate it. A plan usually fails because one of its primary assumptions is wrong. The best way to avoid this is to have others who are qualified review it. Then, with the ego problem solved, listen to them. If the plan is not working, change it or bail out before you lose any more. To change a plan, find out what assumption was wrong and move things around accordingly. If the assumption was critical to the success of the plan, and the plan is not working, it's time to close down. It's always better to take your loss quickly and up front and move on.

Chapter 3
Business Basics

NOTHING
TO WEAR?

TRY THE
BUFFALO EXCHANGE

1072 N. WARREN   795-6499   6305 E. 22ND   790-8350

OPEN SUNDAY FROM 12 TO 5   OPEN LATER EVERYDAY

MONDAY THRU FRIDAY	10 - 6:30
SATURDAY	10 - 6
SUNDAY	12 - 5

FOR THE BEST IN NEW & RECYCLED CLOTHING

Buffalo Exchange Statement of Purpose
(Alias: Mission Statement)
(Alias: Trying to define your reason for being
without making people nauseous)

I do know that we (Buffalo Exchange and all who work with it) are poised for great things. Where to go is getting clear. How to get there is what we all need to work on.

How will we all work on it? That's the fun part—and the hard part.

Some call it a mission statement, which might be a more appropriate term. At any rate, the intent is to give a sense of what it is that we want to do along with the values that we hold as critical components of anything that we do.

It is the purpose of Buffalo Exchange to achieve sustainable profitability, provide a livelihood for its employees, and lead the resale fashion industry by:

Having The Best Clothing At The Best Prices
• Purchasing from and offering to our customers the best in fashionable clothing at the best prices.

Having The Best Workplace
• Providing employees with the best work environment possible with fair compensation and benefits, a business education, and ample opportunities to maximize their contributions and growth and assume responsibility for their decisions and actions.

Acting With Integrity
• Conducting all operations with unflinching integrity and honesty.

Being Flexible And Open
• Maintaining continuous adaptability to change.

Exercising Social Responsibility
- Promoting recycling and reusing as well as all other systems for environmental health.
- Being concerned with and responding to the needs and issues of the communities within which we operate by community involvement and contributions.

Having Fun
- Enjoying what we do and providing enjoyment to all who are involved with us.

Valuing People
- By enjoying the innate goodness and worth of people
- By being thankful for our customers.

30th Anniversary Tour

Competition

My grandmother (a businesswoman in her own right) always said that competition should be dealt with as a blessing.

"Do what you do," she would say, "and do it well. Learn from the competition."

She was a genuinely nice person who never had the sincere urge to strangle any of her siblings. But I still think her advice is good.

Whether it comes from a sibling, or from someone else, competition is always going to be there—appear, disappear, reappear, over and over.

All we can do is to do what we do better and better—learn from them all and stay ahead of the game.

We will need to always work with the basics: Clear purpose, good people, and goodwill.

Spencer's Buby, Rose Block

Christmas Speech, 1990

It's always my job to come here and say something meaningful each year. It requires that I change the mood to serious because that's how "meaningful" tends to be defined by our culture. My mother always used to tell me that I was full of baloney and that she didn't think I'd ever grow up. I thought that was pretty obvious. Besides, it didn't seem very logical to grow up, since, from my limited experience at that tender age, it seemed that the next thing to happen after you grew up was that you died. And to paraphrase Mel Brooks, I try never to do anything that will make me die.

So here we are—all grown up. Buffalo Exchange is mature. It has been around for 18—maybe 19—years. Who's counting anymore? But I don't want it to grow up. Because the next step could be death. You get old, less adventurous, stiff, tired, stubborn, unwilling to try out things, not excited by things. That's old, that's being old, that's being grown up and out. You also get deaf. That's not what we want. That's not what it's about.

Now I'm supposed to thank you for the work you do. I'm supposed to tell you that we all appreciate the job you do. We know the job, we have all done it ourselves, and I want to do that. It's hard work, and you all have done good.

But I want to say something else. I want to say that you better have some fun with it. We all better have some fun with it, or it's over. But keep your eyes and ears open for the symptoms of growing up. Watch out for that old deafness, no one hears what you say. Blindness, no one sees you, or they call you by the wrong name. I do that all the time. My mother would be proud. Refusal to try something different. All the symptoms. Watch out.

Now let's get serious. These are difficult economic times that we are facing. And there is the possibility of war. Let's not forget AIDS—boy that puts the skids on sex.

The Japanese and Germans are buying up everything that is worth anything. So there's a lot to be worried about; and I want you to be concerned and serious. Grow up. Don't joke around with customers—one might have just lost a son in the desert, or in a car accident. Let's not forget MADD—will all designated drivers raise their hands?

What am I saying?

I'm simply saying that in our culture, in our work place, in the work place at large, there are incredible pressures for us to get serious and grow up and get stale and dead. For a business that's death.

How to avoid this? I don't know. I think maybe lots of humor, laughing; that's pretty good. Talking, sharing and communicating, especially with other humans, isn't bad.

What do I want from you? You can help keep Buffalo Exchange from dying by participating in its living. Be our eyes and ears. Don't be so touchy and delicate. This isn't a job for wimps. If your ideas and suggestions are not immediately met with cheers and trumpets, be patient. It won't hurt anything; and it could save us all.

A good company, one that is going to survive and not stagnate and disintegrate, is one in which everyone is talking to everyone and where having a good time and feeling good are considered necessary for staying alive.

So I want you all to be full of baloney. Keep talking, and I wish you all the lightness and silliness of not growing up.

Milton, Dorothy, and
Spencer Block, 1980

Whiners to Winners

Spencer's letter to the company, on the celebration of the 20th Anniversary.

For 20 years, Buffalo Exchange has engaged in a business that we were told had no possibility of survival. "No one buys clothing outright," they said. "You'll be in competition with the established thrift stores like Goodwill and the Salvation Army, and they get their stuff for free." So the advice went in January of 1974.

The idea—no let's call it a vision—was something that no one else had going. It was hard to explain. It dealt with that subtle thing called beauty—fashion—art. I didn't quite get it myself; but I figured I'd go along for the ride. What the hell. We could do it—whatever it was. No problem. Problems were no problem.

The history of the thing is not the point, so we won't get into it. What is important is that we had this idea about ourselves that we were capable and could do anything we needed to do. We could do anything. We had not been brainwashed with the idea that we were somehow not in control of our destinies, that we were the pawns of forces beyond ourselves, that we were, in short, VICTIMS.

Looking back now, I see how foolish we were. After all, Kerstin was (and still is actually) a woman, and a foreigner. I was hair challenged and certainly psychologically disabled due to my eating disorder and my dysfunctional family situation, which was proven by my compulsive overeating. And, to top it off, we were parents without child care. And to even top that off, we had no health insurance. And, even to top that off, we had no money. We were counted among the nation's poor.

The fact that we even bothered to get up in the morning astounds me now that I realize that we were victims of an unjust society—a world that didn't really care for us and would not take care of us.

But we were of another time—a time that is swiftly coming back. This was a time of the can-do people. A time when being a victim was not something to be proud of, when being part of a victimized group was not enough to get you special treatment or just plain money. This was not a time when groups vied with each other to see who could claim to be most victimized. These were the days when not being able was considered the result of personal choice, not outside forces. When people were responsible for their actions and their decisions and could not claim that they were not responsible for their actions because they had just eaten a Twinkie or were caught up in the passion of a riot. It was not a time for the whiners—it was the time of the winners—the can-do people.

This is all part of that can-do, socially responsible mentality that has permeated this company from its beginning. And what we have found is that, lo and behold, even in this day and age, we have some poor foolish souls who still walk around feeling that they are responsible for their own lives and who have positive visions of where they are going and who they are. Who have a confidence and assurance that they can do whatever it takes to make it happen. There still exist among us some can-do people. And here, at Buffalo Exchange, they seem to be flourishing. And there seem to be many.

Company Meeting, 1994

Happy Anniversary

Twenty years in 300 words or less. Minimalism. Fun. Learning always and still. Caring. Loving. Positive life view. Can-do attitude. No victims here. No place for wimps or whiners. Customers and employees are the greatest. Great future: 100 years. Take a breather. Franchising. Management training. Computerization. Socially responsible words. Overpopulation killing the planet. Company must play a part in dealing with:

Competition: I have met the enemy and he is us.

Lessons learned: If you offer great service and great product at a great price, they will beat a path to your door. I'm from Missouri, show me. I'll show you mine if you show me yours. Lives don't change fast. Fast is not what's important. Timing is. Many people don't walk the talk.

Things to try to do: Tell the truth. Ask for what you want. Own your own experiences; don't attribute your emotional state to someone else. Keep your promises, but don't make them lightly. You do it to yourself. Figure out who won't walk the talk or the dog.

Things my parents and grandparents taught me that have been Buffalo proven: Never go to the foot when you can go to the head. Do what you do well and money will come. Do what you love. Love what you do. Love the one you're with. There is a whole, and that's what you keep your eye on. There is good and bad. Be good.

Conclusion: Good prognosis. Great 20. Looking forward to the next. Proud of Kerstin and myself and everything and everyone.

The Hundred Year Strategy

Here are some parts of our strategy to be the best for 100 years. The entire strategy does not exist in one place, and is actually a process.

Desire. We want to be the best for 100 years. Very much. Passionately. Seriously. With lots of affection and fun. Affection and lots of fun. Have affection for living things as well as rocks and air and such. Have affection for FUN. Have affection for JOY.

Experiment and Change. Keep on trying things. Create change and trying out things as an integral part of the company way of being.

Acceptance of Reality. When trying new things, be realistic. Deal with the need to make money. This also relates to the refusal to accept fads and fast talking B.S. as truth.

Respect for and understanding of:
- the environment
- the individuals
- living things
- those things that support our lives

Bulldog Persistence. Never stop trying to be the best. Never give up or operate outside of the framework of your basic principles—the ones you just know are true and right.

Enjoy it. If it ain't fun, why do it?

Spencer, 2006

Chapter 4
Company Culture

Company Culture • 63

The 30th Anniversary Tour

It began as a simple idea: For our 30th Anniversary (which actually was January 15th of 2004) we would visit every single one of the 30 stores in 30 days in this 31st year of our existence. One look at the map and the mileage chart, and after some simple calculations, we realized that would not be possible. We decided to do it in stages—south in the cold months, north in the warm months.

We then thought of how much fun it would be to take our little Scamp travel trailer along. We could dress it up and stay in it as we went around the country. This we actually did do.

The fantasy and the reality were a little different. Trailer courts and campgrounds can run from seedy to fantastic, and we stayed at both and all levels in between—from exquisite pine forests to treeless scraped and bladed sand lots surrounded by huge fuel storage tanks. We experienced a slice of Americana that exposed a varied and vibrant country full of contradictions and beauty.

Montgomery, Alabama, was a perfect example. From its sleepy central city to its modern shopping malls, it boasts being the "Cradle of the Confederacy" at the same time it sees itself as the "birthplace of the Civil Rights movement." It's home to the little church where Martin Luther King preached, now a shrine for social activists.

In Pennsylvania, we had flat tires   In Virginia, we saw Manassas—the site of the Civil War battle where on July 21, 1861, 900 men died and changed the nature of how Americans viewed that war.

We saw all the stores. What became evident as we went from one location to the next was that there was a standard— an average—from which to make comparisons. There were differences in emotional climates, inventories, physical plants, etc. Sometimes these differences were substantial; but seeing all the stores in rapid succession gave a sense for what the middle ground was, and it was a level of excellence that put us at the top of our industry and surpassed our past performance. We are better now than ever before.

So this tour came to be a private seminar on America and Buffalo Exchange. In both, we experienced variety, vitality, and strength. No, the average Buffalo Exchange employee is not just like the average American. But in meeting and talking to so many of both, it seemed that the important things—basic values, goals, and desires—were similar and cut from the same cultural fabric. Americans are a good-hearted, open, accepting people. They are generally enthusiastic and optimistic. The stereotype holds true for the people as a whole. The same is true of Buffalo Exchange employees, and of Buffalo Exchange as a company. We have borrowed some of the best aspects of this culture as our guiding principles.

Our travels were exhausting, invigorating, educational, and rewarding on many levels. We came away from it all with a deep sense of pride for what we have been privileged to participate in, an appreciation for the labors of all those who have helped and are helping to make it work, and renewed gratitude for the fact that (whatever its faults) we live in a country that enables such things to happen.

Halloween pumpkin carving contest, 2004

Those Among Us

There are those among us
Who show us through their being
That we have the possibility of goodness.

Who in their vision of themselves and others hold a
golden sphere of warmth and caring.
They are the other side of terror, warriors against evil,
protectors of kindness and nurture.

They are often unnoticed in their beauty and holiness.
But what is most rare is to know one and call him
or her "friend," even though it is so easy; for they rejoice
in you and help you to be your better self.

They accept you as you are and honor you that way.
They are courageous; because they do not what is easy
and comfortable for them, but often what is difficult
because it is needed.

They are in every people, in every culture.
They exist as part of the human condition over and over
again through the shameful history of our species,
shining out of the masses as little sparks of what we
know to be go(o)d.

And they shall always
be there among us.

McKenzie Harrison
Buffalo Exchange model

Exercise

Kerstin and I have walked just about every morning for the last 20 years. We now exercise and then walk at a nice talking pace for 45 minutes—2.2 miles as measured by my GPS. We walk out our door and into a mountain park.

On our walks, we get to see great sunrises, deer, javelina, coyotes, rattlesnakes, desert tortoises, tons of bugs of every kind, cacti and all form of desert vegetation blooming and fruiting—all of nature's fantastic gifts and glories.

Has it helped us in business? Who knows? Maybe.

Maybe we think more clearly and understand our place in the Universe a little better. Maybe it helps us to accept the insanity of government regulations combined with abusive employees with magnanimity and peace. Maybe it makes for a happier workplace.

Who knows? If nothing else, it has been lots of fun.

The other day, there were blotches of meager rain clouds at sunrise as we walked. The rich orange colors of the eastern sunrise silhouetted the mountains and saguaros. The sun broke through at a fantastic angle and lit up one of the surrounding mountains in a gold color to the north. Then, to the west, it began to rain and a double rainbow formed. Can you start a bad day like this?

Kerstin and Zillie on their morning walk

Each Day

Each day as it comes
We join hands
And walk out into the sunshine

We beam
And talk gently to a universe
That hears not

But turns those small breaths
Into roses at some other time
And connects us

To other days that will come

Spencer and Kerstin, 2007

The Love of Fashion

A business should have a core, a heart. This is what drives it. This is what directs its decisions and actions. Buffalo Exchange is a company started by a fashion hound. We grew a customer base of clothing addicts who were fashion aficionados in their own right. We traded—rather we shared a love of clothing and accessories, and it was this symbiotic love affair that cemented us together over decades of mutual admiration.

In the year 2000, Buffalo Exchange directed its "X Team" to continue to try to come up with new ideas and focus. The "X Team" with the addition of myself drove to Rocky Point (Puerto Penasco), Mexico, for a think-tank retreat.

The team met for three days. In the daytime, we sat and talked, took long walks on the beach, and talked some more. At night, we went into town for dinner, drank, tried Karaoke at another local place, came back to the beach house, played board games, talked more, and then slept.

The sand, beach, and beer were not having a very dynamic effect. Actually, it seemed to be acting as a sedative along with the general sedative effect of Mexico itself. The next day was the same general routine. The team was made up of myself, —Spencer—Rebecca, an area manager, a store manager, our marketing director, our arts director, and a franchise owner.

Up until the last day, nothing much happened. There were no new ideas that seemed to grab anyone's imagination. However, throughout the whole time, there were some common threads that seemed to be taking hold.

One of these—perhaps the simplest one— was the concept of FASHION.

Buffalo Exchange, it became obvious, has always dealt with fashion. Although, at first mention, a simple idea, the obvious nature of it belied the fact that it was a very significant discovery.

It seemed at the time that a group whose mandate was to come up with some ingenious and significant ways to change our business to make us the number one re-seller in the world should be coming up with something more dynamic and exciting than the simple thought that we deal with fashion. After returning to this simple idea time and time again, it finally sank in: FASHION IS WHAT WE ARE ALL ABOUT. That was the great discovery. This was the great re-invention that had to happen.

This was what we strayed from over the years. It wasn't customer service. It wasn't better training, or better management, or better selection of employees. It wasn't the latest method of business creativity. It was simply fashion. That was our driver. That was what we knew. That was where we came from and where we would be going.

Everything else involved ways of getting there. But fashion was "there." This was the magnificent revelation of what lay deep within the core of our existence. This was our heart and soul. FASHION. When I came back to Tucson and shared with Kerstin our great revelation, she looked at me in a slightly puzzled way.

"I knew that," she said flatly and returned to her office.

X Team, 2000

Buffalo Gal

Buffalo Gal, you worked hard all day
Buffalo Gal, now it's time to play
You've done all you needed to do
So drink a beer, come on, have two

Buffalo Gal, you work so hard it seems
But that's ok
I think it's in the genes
Yours like to get up and run
Mine look for food and fun

You took us all a long long way
Pushin' rags and makin' hay
Still you never blinked an eye

Lover, mother, my best friend
Honest heart to the very end
Never whined and never one to cry

So Buffalo Gal, you worked hard all day
Buffalo Gal, now it's time to play
So drink your beer, come on, have two
But that's all

Cause there's still a lot to do
And honey, I'm stuck on you

A Short & Personal
30-Year Retrospective

This company was made what it is by people who got up every morning (or every afternoon, depending) and came to work to do what needed to be done. Most of them got a kick out of what they did and who they did it with. Most of them put their heart into it.

Memory can blur a bit over time; and so we fill in the gaps and sharpen up the images with our own mental versions of Adobe® Photoshop®. Here's mine.

Buffalo Exchange was a fantasy at its inception. It was a simple idea that was exquisitely executed with affection, appreciation, and a whole lot of fun. It has been kept alive all these years with those same simple emotions which have grown stronger and stronger with time.

The affection was at the beginning. Affection for the fashion, for the people involved on both sides of the counter, and for the new freedom that it gave to those of us who had worked for others and other institutions.

The appreciation came from a deep and experiential understanding of how fortunate we were to be able to do what we liked doing and actually put food on our table, and eventually on the tables of hundreds and hundreds of people through the years. I am proud of that.

The gratitude also always has extended to thousands upon thousands of individuals who came across the thresholds of our stores to work and/or to shop. They made it what it is. We have never forgotten that plain fact.

Some of them became the stories and legends in their own time—the fashion-passion addicted, the quarrelers, the pickers and the picky, the philosophers, the thieves, the Sikhs, the bakers, the candle stick makers—all our brothers and sisters in commerce, in life. They taught us. And you taught us. We learned. It was the University of the Buffalo.

We earned our MBAs the fun way. The fun was just always there. It was part of our nature and the nature of you all, and it became an integral part of everything we did. Perhaps because of our ignorance and naiveté, we never understood why business had to be serious. In the beginning, we had no goal other than to try to make a living and survive.

Later, we decided that it would be a good thing to try to build a good company that could last a hundred years. We felt if we could sustain a company with morals—one that operated in a fair and socially responsible manner—that would be a worthwhile accomplishment. And we believed it would give us a perspective that would go beyond short-term profits and small-minded thinking. Although we have not always functioned with this goal in the forefront of our minds, it has shaped the general way we approach our management of the company. It's a big enough goal that has allowed us to continue our haphazard dance with time with the energy and enthusiasm that such a journey requires.

I end this retrospective with the words of Robert Frost that somehow express my sense about this incredible journey.

> *"I shall be telling this with a sigh*
> *Somewhere ages and ages hence;*
> *Two roads diverged in a wood, and I—*
> *I took the one less traveled by,*
> *And that has made all the difference."*
> —Robert Frost,
> *The Road Not Taken*, 1916

I want to thank all of you for one hell of a great ride.

Chapter 5
Giving Back

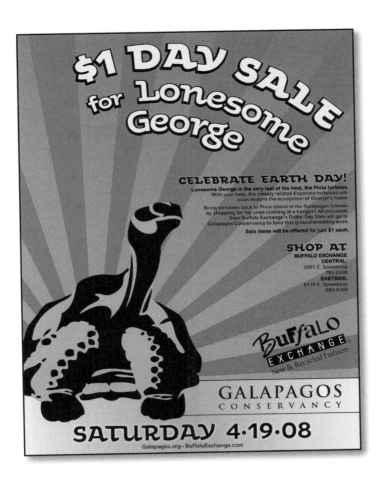

Celebrating the Arts

Spencer, 1950

Once, when I was a kid cleaning out cat scat in a dark, four-foot crawl space under a fish store, I came across these words scratched and penciled into one of the wooden support poles. My eyes were better then. Under the dim light bulb I made out this: "you readin this, pity you sory ass."

Later, after a couple of hours crouched in that hot, dark space with dried cat poop dust choking me through my bandana-wrapped mouth and nose, I crawled up the stairs into the light and air of the store and sat. Then, I mulled over that note and what it had said—or what I believe it said. My translation was, "If you're reading this, I pity your sorry ass." But his—and I have always assumed that, in those days, only a boy would have been sent down to do this job— his was the better use of words.

What a wonderful thing to leave behind. A fellow in labor had taken time to greet me, to leave me an understanding of our condition, the condition of "sorry-ass." And that's exactly what I felt like at that moment. He comforted me across time. He was an emerging artist, no doubt. At the very least he was a contributor to the arts—a poet.

Art is not a luxury. Art is not something that humans do when they have nothing else to do. Art is an essential part of the human condition. It happens everywhere and in all circumstances. It has happened in caves, on islands, on mountains. It happens in war, in peace, in sadness and in happiness. It is written, etched, tattooed, sung, chanted, recited, molded, acted, painted. It's a great pair of shoes, a wonderful dress, or a fantastic pair of earrings.

It is our way of expressing our wonderment, our understanding or lack of it, our spirituality, our recognition of our mortality and immortality. It is the single piper slowly joined note for note by the flute and then the fiddle—joining and giving sustenance to each other. It is a lonely notation in a dusty crawl space below a fish store. It is not a luxury. It is not an option. It is not frosting on the cake. It is not whipped cream on the sundae. It is the cake and the sundae, and all that. It's the whole enchilada. It is the essence of who we are. It is the representation of our existence.

The Buffalo Exchange Arts Award was created because we, the founders, believe this. It was created to celebrate the arts and those individuals who live it one way or another. And today, we are here to do just that.

We continue our long tradition of contributing to the communities that have supported us. We have dedicated funds for the arts and for one true group of victims in our society—the animals that are misused and abused.

We thought long and hard about this giving. Where should we put our money? What was the responsible thing to do? What made sense for Buffalo Exchange? What we realized was that we are part of the arts. We also realized that the arts are what enable a society to see beyond its everyday experience. Artists are the visionaries. They go where no one has gone and show us the way. Often we don't want to see what they are showing us. They can make us uncomfortable. But artists are essential to the well-being of our society.

So, notwithstanding everything from Amnesty International to the African Wildlife Foundation, we chose to give our major funding to artists and animals.

In Tucson, Buffalo Exchange has donated $25,000 for the initial creation of the Buffalo Exchange Arts Fund* which, beginning in the spring of next year and each year thereafter, will grant a $10,000 award to an individual artist in the performing or visual arts for work that is excellent and innovative. This is a no-strings award, which, incidentally, has no relationship to victim status. It does not consider financial need or anything other than the quality of the work produced.

* The Buffalo Exchange Arts Fund was created in 1994.

Lonesome George

This is the ballad of Lonesome George
The last turtle of his kind

It's a song of how it came to be
That George got left behind

It all started a million years ago or so
When George's group was doing just fine
Then the humans came with their hungry ways
And found that turtles were fine to dine

The old sailing ships that needed meat
Took the turtles live and kept them neat
On their backs for up to a year
With no food or water

And so they slowly took all there was
As we humans are wont to do
And finally there was only Lonesome George
And one or two in a zoo

So George's genes are now all that's left
Of this ancient breed of life
We squeezed the turtles like we've squeezed the planet
And drained it of its life

But there is a chance that in this life
We may yet make some repair
By putting tortoises back on islands
That are our trust and care

So help us out
Give it your best
Stop the stuffing and the gorge
And back the drive
To bring it back alive
In the name of Lonesome George

Taking a Stand

Taking stands for causes that one believes in is a noble activity that Buffalo Exchange supports, in principle.

As I have stated before, it is my firm belief that overpopulation is the primary cause of all of the world's current disasters, both ecological and political.

Do the company owners have the right to use the company's name to support causes and organizations that not all employees might support? In my opinion, we do. But the consequences of such actions need to be considered. Who will be alienated? What if we cause a store to be picketed and thus become unprofitable?

Not only this, but we are striving for a situation in which employees can identify with and feel positive about the company they work for, can feel a part of that company.

Does taking stands on controversial issues put this goal in jeopardy?

At this time, the company as a whole is primarily taking a stand on issues relating to overpopulation and ecology. Currently, company policy also prohibits store managers from putting up political and/or issue-related posters, announcements, and petitions that have not been approved by Area Managers and, in theory, top management. The idea, of course, is to keep from having Buffalo Exchange in political alignment with or in support of causes not endorsed by us.

Is this right? Does anyone care? I hope so. There's certainly enough calamity going on to invigorate even the most apathetic of us.

Chapter 6
Know Yourself

THIS MAN WANTS YOUR CLOTHES!

He will pay cash.

BUFFALO EXCHANGE

• **buying** • **trading** • **selling**

The Best in New & Recycled Clothing

Loyalty

All these years I have been involved in this business, I have never used the term "loyalty" or even thought much about it. It always seemed to me that loyalty was something I had no right to ask of an employee. After all, I reasoned, I pay and the employee works. That's the deal. What the employee does on her own time is her business, etc.

Then I saw the error of my ways. I realized that this company has established a loyalty that it gives to its employees and that this requires a response in kind. More than that, in order to survive and flourish, the company has to encourage loyalty and commitment on the part of its employees.

In this light, I have begun to see that gossiping wildly and wickedly—sowing seeds of discontent through the gossip line instead of through the available feedback channels which allow for true progress and change—that these disruptive and subtle activities of disrespect did the company harm and therefore did harm to the people who spent so much of their lives making this company happen. I have come to realize that my passive acceptance of these activities was harmful as well.

When individuals would share discontent at the store level or in a department at G/A [General Administration] but fail to disclose any names or specifics, even though their goal was to share such information and encourage management to react, I used to listen and accept. What I should have done was thrown that person out of my office.

Hell, if you know about trouble, it is your duty to tell all you know if your loyalties are truly with the company. If not, then what the hell are you doing here? Go work someplace where you can be true. I don't want you here. That's probably what I should have said, but I didn't. I should have. I will from now on.

This company gives a lot. A lot is expected in return. To allow the saying of half-truths, pointless complaining, and outright hostile diatribes enables and encourages disrespect and demoralization. It is important for me to share that people who choose to engage in such activities are not allowed to continue to work for the company. Honest and open disagreements are acceptable and necessary for a healthy business. Closed back-room backbiting and complaining are not.

Spencer and Vella Austin, Buffalo
Exchange Chief Operations Officer, 1996

The Matrix: Mind-Shifting

Managing and cancer came into a different focus for me the other day. I had to make a decision about my health—mental as well as physical. That decision somehow got me thinking about the last discussion I had with store managers at the last training session concerning walking that fine line between being an approachable, compassionate, and understanding manager and being a strong, courageous, and sensible leader. The former seemed to be an easier side of the line, since the people one manages are the same folks one spends the bulk of their waking hours with; and we, as social beings, have a natural tendency to be "friendly" with those we spend the most time with.

My own situation was framed differently, but dealt with one key element of commonality—defining who we are. I often joke that I had no idea of who I really was or what I really wanted to spend my time doing until I was 50. Of course, that's an exaggeration; but it does point out a simple truth: that, for most of us, knowing ourselves is a life-long pursuit that can and probably should continue to the end.

In my case, one of the blessings of cancer was that it forced me into a stark reality check about what I was about; what I loved and how I defined myself and how I could re-define myself. In other words, I was forced to see aspects of myself that I had been able to avoid looking at. I had to acknowledge and experience great terror and great compassion. I had to deal with a body that was not doing at all what I wanted it to do—a body that was not totally in my control anymore. Great shocks in life cause these sorts of adjustments. Car accidents that leave people incapacitated, loss of a loved one, or loss of some valued possession such as a house or all one's money— all of these can force this reassessment of who we are and what really counts for us. I believe that new store managers experience similar life adjustments, although perhaps to a lesser degree. It is true for any of us when placed in new situations that force us to review and possibly modify our concept of who we are and what we are capable of.

Store managers have to come to terms with a new set of realities when they take over a store. They suddenly have to know about a new set of business-related intricacies: the physical plant, protocols of communication, inventory control, people management, etc.

But hardest of all, they have to learn to walk that fine line between being a social being and a boss, between being an approachable, friendly individual and a person who manages the doings of other people in the workplace, giving direction and making decisions that affect the lives of others. Going too far in either direction puts the new manager—even older more experienced managers—in the vacuum of ineffectiveness. "Too much a friend leads to the end. Too much a witch, you're in the ditch."

One thing for sure, a store manager cannot have a staff of friends. You should keep and cultivate friends outside of the staff you supervise. It's part of a survival technique. Re-define yourself. Understand this limitation on who you now are. If you don't, you're likely to end up with a store full of friends over whom you have no authority.

Being a store manager—being the key person in determining whether or not a store will survive and prosper—can be a life-changing experience that forces a person to confront who they really are and what their real talents are. It creates an occasion for making choices. It forces the questions: Is this for me? Do I really want to do this? Can I do this? Or not.

Many who have failed have gone on their way without the slightest insight into why things did not work out. They have simplistic answers ranging from a bad location to a bad company that did not give them enough training, love, support, time (take your pick or mix and match). But they learned nothing about themselves and who they are.

Back to my path that split—the choice of which way to go and the most recent re-defining of self that was required. I was not in New Orleans for this last May's managers meeting. I could have attended this meeting; but it would have put me at risk, since it happened at a time when my immune system was impaired due to medical treatment. In addition, I would not have been in top physical condition. My horizon had shrunk. I was now a person who had this limitation. The reality of me is changing. Who am I now? What can I do and not do? What do I want to do and not do? This is a time to re-define myself, whether I like it or not—whether I want to or not.

My reality is that I am a person who has great opportunity to utilize his time embracing a world of activities that I am passionate about.

What I cannot do is clear. I cannot walk my two-mile walk every day, only some days. I cannot work on certain days. I can't travel at certain times, etc.

What I can do that I love is still enough for many lifetimes of doing. When I don't see this new reality clearly, much like a store manager who has not had a mind shift that recognizes a new reality, I spend time doing things that I do not enjoy and am not good at. I get depressed. I see the glass as half empty. I see myself as a directionless feather being blown by the wind. I fail to see my power and my opportunities. I engage in useless repetitive behavior. And I fail to make choices that are good for me in the new reality that I am not seeing.

The good news is that the problem described is easy to remedy. Just open your eyes and look around. Ask those basic questions. Are you happy? Do you like what you are doing? Do you wake up full of fun and enthusiastic anticipation? Well, I don't do that every day either.

But I do most of the time. And it's most of the time that counts. If the simple answer to these questions is yes, then you are probably in the right place at the right time doing the right thing. If the answer is a definite and robust no, then open your eyes and take a good look at yourself and at the reality of the situation you are in. As with all solutions, the answer may be simple; but getting there can be hard work.

Tito Haggardt and Spencer, 2000

Follow Your Bliss

Spencer and granddaughter Melissa,
with a stone seal at Friday Harbor

Joseph Campbell taught and wrote about mythology. He gained some notoriety before his death by way of a TV series with Bill Moyers. But what's important for my purposes here is that when asked by Bill Moyers in an interview what advice he gave to his students, he replied that he told them to go with the bliss. I personally think that that is a profound piece of advice.

It doesn't mean to be selfish. It doesn't mean to ignore your responsibility to others. It simply means to make decisions based on what it is you love.

To be happy, you have to make the right decisions in life.

Decision making is a cumulative affair. The right ones add up as do the wrong ones until you either find yourself in self-defeating or self-enhancing situations.

You cannot follow the bliss, cannot make good decisions without self-knowledge.

How do you find out who you really are? Well, some lucky ones just know. The rest of us have to work at it. Or not. It starts by seriously asking the question. If you don't ask the question, the odds of getting at the answer are pretty slim.

The Zen Approach: What's the question? That's the

question. Who am I? What am I capable of? There are many questions, but one I suggest is: What do I love? Not Who, but What.

Romantic love, although dominating our culture, is not a very reliable road to happiness. I'm not knocking it; but let me say that if you are presently madly in love with someone, your progress in the pursuit of self-awareness will have to wait awhile, be put on the backburner until a semblance of reality returns to your life.

The love I am talking about is a very basic attraction that you have to certain aspects of living. I will say only that one road to the truth of who you are is the path of your passions: those things that give you a sense of happiness and well-being, a sense of competency and enjoyment. These constitute the bliss. These are the guideposts.

The best advice I know of: "Follow Your Bliss."

Spencer, ca. 2000

The Center of the Universe

Spencer and Kerstin in Hawaii

You are the center of the universe whether you accept it or not. You need to know who you are in this existence, or your universe becomes very confusing.

This is not a selfish position to assume: It is simply a truth, a knowledge—the most important knowing there is—the knowledge of yourself and who you are.

You need to engage in the world of work with this knowledge. Most failures in the world of work are due to a lack of understanding what will make you happy.

You may get what you thought you wanted. But without making money, your business will fail. You did not love it enough.

How to know who you are. (Good Luck!)

Pay attention to all the little things that give you joy. Odds are, these are the kinds of things you should be doing to make a living. Cleaning, organizing, gossiping.

The trick is to find areas in the world of work that require these kinds of things.

Some of this can be deeply psychological; but before you get too carried away with the psychology of it, pay attention to what is right in front of your face—you and your joys.

This is what will tell you who you are and what you need to be doing. As far as managing people, **stay away from managing people** if you have a profile that includes a heavy emphasis on:

- Needing people to like you.
- Pleasing others and having a hard time saying no.
- Focusing more on people than on things.
- Liking to become involved in the problems and the personal lives of the people you manage.

If you need people to approve or like you, managing people may not be the right job for you, especially if you are overly concerned with what people may think of you. If this is the case, it is better to choose a solitary profession such as writing or accounting or cabinet-making. Be a plumber, welder, astrophysicist, but do not place yourself in a position of managing people. You will be happier.

Swami Buffalo

A manager asks: "Swami Buffalo, how can I gain the respect of my subordinates? And while I'm at it, how about my parents?"

Swami says: "Forget about your parents. We don't have that kind of time. As far as respect of others, always think before you respond to any communication that makes you hesitate or makes your bowels feel peculiar. Bowels are very very important indicators of danger, not just overindulgence. You do not want your bowels in an uproar. Uproarious bowels lead to flatulence, which in turn will lead to a loss of face, since most faces will turn away, especially in confined spaces. [This is actually the derivation of the expression 'losing face'.] This will definitely result in a loss of respect. So, not answering immediately can help relax your psychological being, your buffic energy and your bowels.

Practice saying such things as, I'll have to get back to you about that. Or, I'll have to think about that.

This will not be seen as a sign of weakness but rather an indication of great intelligence and wisdom. And even if you are not that intelligent or wise, most people cannot tell the difference."

Self-Perception

Who am I anyway?

Goal: My goal is to help you get some notion of how your view of who you are affects others and determines how you negotiate the many paths through your existence.

This probably sounds self-evident, but there is more to it than what appears at first glance.

We all have views of who we are. Some of these are realistic, meaning that they coincide with or at least take into consideration what others see, and that they have some relevance to how you are able to interact with the world at large. Of course, realistic is a relative term; but if we are to proceed at all, we will simply have to concede that in this context it refers to an approximation that we can all agree to.

We are all aware that an individual whose view of himself is too far from reality is generally dysfunctional and regarded as nuts, insane, bonkers, etc.

One of the concepts I will posit here is that most of us, although not insane, have fairly unrealistic views of who we are and what we are capable of.

Somehow, we manage, for the most part, to function. Sometimes, some of us periodically stop being functional. I will also posit here that substance abuse, eating disorders, nervous breakdowns and the like are all results of self-views that are incongruent with reality. An excellent example of this would be a case of anorexia in which the anorexic individual would look in the mirror and see herself as too fat.

So aside from being functional, why should you care who you really are? Why?

So. . .you. . .can. . .be. . .happy.

Now, there is an assumption being made here that is very important to examine. The assumption is that underneath all the layers of accumulated behavior, we are perfectly wonderful, magnificent beings, and that seeing this truth will liberate us and allow us to maximize our existence. Something like that.

Well, why is that so hard to believe? I find it ironic that the same people who watch an eagle in flight and get tears in their eyes for the magnificence of it can then look at themselves or other human beings and very often not be struck by the absolute majesty of who we truly are. We are marvelous. We are amazing creatures. And I believe that as we peel the layers off and learn who we are, that we will be amazed at the goodness and the beauty that we find.

We are social animals—the most social of all—and it is in our nature to be nurturing and supportive of one another.

So, back to the other reason for getting to know yourself: **to be better at what you do.**

Spencer playing with the Mt. Lemmon
Marching Mandolin Band

Feed Me

The Cherokee Legend Of Two Wolves

This little story was enclosed with a Christmas greeting card, and it goes like this:

One evening, an old Cherokee told his grandson about a battle that goes on inside people. He said, "My son, the battle is between two 'wolves' inside us all.

One is evil: it is anger, envy, jealousy, sorrow, regret, greed, arrogance, self-pity, guilt, resentment, inferiority, lies, false pride, superiority, and ego.

The other is good: it is joy, peace, love, hope, serenity, humility, kindness, benevolence, empathy, generosity, truth, compassion and, faith."

The grandson thought about it for a minute, and then asked his grandfather, "Which one wins?"

The old Cherokee simply replied, "The one you feed."

Chapter 7
Leadership

Welcome to the Buffalo Exchange School for Business Literacy

Nowadays I meet with economic advisers, accountants, estate planners, bankers, etc.

I remember my first such meeting around 25 years ago. The consultant asked me what my main motivation for being in business was. After a few seconds of deep thought, I responded with the only thing that I knew was true: "Eating," I said. "Putting food on the table."

And that's about it, folks. That's what it's all about. I have always been happy that I made enough to have a roof over my head and food on my table. I come from a people—refugees from Eastern Europe and the Steppes of Asia—who valued that above all else. And after that, they valued learning.

So, did I learn anything? After 30 years, what do I know?

A couple of things. First, that the *Wizard of Oz* is a great movie. It's got all the trials and tribulations of life on target. Heart, brains, courage, belief, optimism, persistence, and, finally, wisdom—all the things you need to make a good management stew, all the things you need to make a good person, all the things you need to make a good company.

Another thing I learned is that management theories and systems come and go, and you have to take from them what you can and let the rest fade away. Out of all the gleanings from these systems, the one that seems to have stood the test of time is the five golden rules of successful human interaction. All five require elements of oz – courage, heart, brains, etc.

Here's how I think of them:

1. Take responsibility for yourself – for your actions, your decisions, and your life. Do less and you will be less.

2. Speak the truth, always with respect.

3. Keep your agreements. Most problems between a company and its employees have to do with this not being done by either party.

4. Ask for what you want. Say what you mean. Contrary to what the *X-Files* might imply, most of us are not mind readers.

5. Be here, now. The hardest. The most elusive. The highest order of being. LIVE IN THE PRESENT. We approach it when we give 100% attention to each individual we deal with and to what we are doing.

So that's it. That's the accummulated knowledge of 30 years of living in business. Do I do all these things? Of course not. But I know better.

Spencer in his home office, 2008

A Dialogue

I received this note from a concerned manager:

As a result of a conversation I had with another manager, I thought I would pass along this observation on your analogy about getting old. I found it very interesting and applicable to how we run the stores, but it is possible that the younger managers might have missed the point, because this is not something that they have experienced firsthand yet. They quite possibly didn't grasp what you intended. I was thinking you might be able to put the point across more forcefully if you used something they do have a clear understanding of—say, fashion. If you were to suggest that the stores have to remain adaptable by not getting stuck in certain styles, you might get the point across to them.

My answer:

Dear Anonymous,

I agree that my analogy about getting old is probably out of reach for many people who have never known an old person, something that happens quite frequently in our society. I also think that plain talk is sometimes better that circumventing the heart of the thing with stories and analogies.

I think your point is well taken in that I don't really have to worry about the store managers stagnating. That can happen as one ages or to those long enough in a job to crystallize. The concern I had about the company losing its creative edge has to do with those of us who are older, have been here longer, and need to be prodded a little along the way—maybe even moved out of the way sooner or later. And what I was really doing was simply asking for help.

Help us stay forever young. Do this by continuing the ongoing dialogue—by participating—by thinking.

The Wizard of Oz

I have used the movie *The Wizard of Oz* for years to teach managers how to manage. It is a fine blend of the basic characteristics that all good managers should have: courage, heart, brains, and persistence to move onward. The same principles hold for the entrepreneur.

What the wizard teaches:

Courage: Like the lion. It is lonely at the top. It is supposed to be. Business is not a democracy.

You are the boss, the leader, the director, the major planner, the big kahuna.

1. No strength of character will lead to chaos and unhappy employees. Saying "no" is often necessary. If you say "yes" to everyone, no one will be happy.
2. You are not there to win a popularity contest; you are there to manage.
3. If you are desperate for the approval of others, management is not a good place for you.

Heart: Like the Tin Man. Compassion and caring are essential to good management. People respond to these.

Brains: Intelligence like the Scarecrow. Manage with your common sense. If it does not sound right, it very well may not be. Be smart. Work smart. Working hard is ok, when necessary; but it is not a replacement for working smart. Use your intelligence.

Persistence: Like Dorothy. Dorothy never gave up. She pushed on through lions and tigers and bears.

1. Keeping on keeping on is important.
2. When your employees do not wear their name tags, you can get them to do it.
3. You have to believe that you can.
4. You have to see the end goal and be committed to it.

Above all you must balance these elements. Too much heart or too much logic or too much courage will not work. They must be in harmony with each other. Balance so that not one becomes the dominant characteristic.

Courage: Being too brazen.

Heart: Yes to every whimper.

Brains: Everything by logic; by the book. No flexibility.

Persistence: Stubbornness and lack of listening.

Leadership Is...

1. Leadership is the process of influencing people to achieve a common goal.

2. Leadership is the art of being.

The first definition is the formal definition. That's the definition that seems to say it all.

The second definition is not as clear, but, I would argue, has more truth to it. That is the Tao (or Zen, if you will) definition of Leadership: the one that tries to approach the reason why some lead and others cannot.

Leadership positions are not the place for lost or needy souls. What we will try to do is give you a sense of what leadership is—not a definition, but a keen awareness—and hopefully give you some tools that you can use once you have the "being" part of the process pinned down.

For management people in our company, leadership has to involve accepting, embracing, and clearly and strongly standing for what it is we do, how we do it, and the basic morality that we espouse. One word that almost always shows a non-leadership mentality is the word "they." "They" want us to do it this way. That's the way "they" want it. "They" are going to ... The leadership word is either "I" or "we."

There is leadership for the good and leadership for the bad. I think Hitler was bad. I think Gandhi was good. So, just because you lead does not automatically make you good.

There are leaders who are appointed—who get there by position—and leaders who emerge more naturally out of human interactions. In your situations, you better hope that you are the leader of your group. When the appointed leader does not lead, someone else will. That can be your problem employee, your Store Secretary/Bookkeeper (SSB), your assistant, or whoever. If it's not you, you're in trouble.

Often, when that happens, we refer to it as "going native." That's when the driving force of the group in question is not the common goal, but rather the chaotic and conflicting goals of all the individuals involved, disintegrating into an operational and moral failure. Humans need leadership.

Different Styles

There is the myth of the dynamic, bombastic, charismatic leader—the Donald Trump jerk leader. This is the common mistake that people make when thinking about leadership. There are all kinds of personalities who lead, from the mild-mannered Gandhi type to the more dynamic Churchill or Roosevelt types. We get our ideas from politics; but the reality of leadership is that it is done by a huge variety of people who serve on school boards, run businesses, and unfortunately fight in wars. Some speak loudly, some don't.

Why is Dorothy the leader in *The Wizard of Oz*? Why is the Dali Lama a leader?

There are, some commonalities to all of them.

Common Aspects: You can cut the cheesecake a million ways or more. It will still be cheesecake. This is just one way of looking at leadership.

Four Aspects: What leaders do.

1. Command the vision. Understand it. Embrace it. Own it. If you can't tell me the vision you have for this company and especially for your store or department, then I can't help you. I have one for this company: To be the best damn company in the world. To have, the best employees, the best customers, the best inventory at the best prices in our stores, the cleanest bathrooms, the cleanest vacuum cleaner bags, the best places to work, and to survive and keep it alive

Milton Block

because it's a good thing that earns people a living and does good things for the world. That's just off the cuff. If you want, I could spend a few months with a group of you to come up with a perfect one; but I just gave you the one that's in my heart. That's the one you want to hear. That's the kind of vision you have to have to lead anyone anywhere. Who wants to follow a dead horse? Or to follow nothing at all?

2. Make it clear. Leaders make it understandable. They communicate it so their intentions are clear.

3. Leaders are trustworthy. They speak the truth. They keep promises. They are consistent. Once the trust is gone or shaken, the ability to influence is weakened. My dad was a fishmonger—a leader. He built his own business. (I have to get him in here, because he will soon be forgotten; and we just passed All-Saints Day—the Day of the Dead. So I have been thinking about some of his teachings lately.) Anyway, he taught me that my word was a very precious thing. Never give it quickly or without due thought. Once given, always keep it. My biggest troubles have always been giving it too quickly and then having to keep it. One of the key components to his success was keeping his word to everyone—the big and the small.

4. Leaders manage themselves. There is a center to them. They project a sense of knowing who they are. They tend to be able to step outside of their own selves and see clearly what is happening and how it is happening. They understand their skills, their strengths and weaknesses, and they are therefore able to navigate through and around them. They nurture their strengths. They take risks and are able to accept their failures as steps toward success. They are their own cheerleaders.

Sustainable leadership enables others and spawns leaders rather than followers and personal glory.

Leadership can be learned; but only through experience. The first time you say no and are not struck down by lightening is both a frightening and yet very liberating experience.

If you abdicate the leadership role, someone else will take it over. When we say that a store "goes native" that is what has happened: the leadership role has been taken over by someone besides the manager.

There can be more than one leader at a time, but it needs to be a carefully choreographed dance with clear duties and powers and communication. It seldom works.

Buffalo Exchange End of the Year
Awards Dinner, 2009

The Tao of Leadership

Leadership is an act that consists of two major parts: showing and deciding.

Showing is based on "being." You are what you are. That's what shows.

To lead, you must be outside of yourself to see what is happening.

To see clearly, you must divest yourself of self-interest as much as possible to get a sense of why it is happening.

To lead, you must show and always be the LEADER:

- Not the follower
- Not the friend
- Not the caretaker
- Not the most clever or quickest

To lead, you must show you are:

- The one who has taken on the task of showing the way
- The one who knows where everyone is going
- The one who must say both yes and no
- The one whose role can only be known by other leaders
- The one who stands alone

To "be" is to know who you are in all times and places. The less you change from time and place to time and place, the more you are being. A leader should "be." When this is the case, others will know this.

Being cancels out the concern of status or regard. It is both of these given by you to yourself. As you seek these, you lose them. They cannot be sought after. As you approach them, they escape, because there is nowhere for them to reside. When you have a place for them, they will come of their own accord and settle within you. Much as a shy cat who settles on your lap when you are at peace.

The second part of leadership is deciding:
- Always let it be known that you are the one who decides
- Always let it be known that you listen and consider the input of others
- By listening. By telling them.

It is best to decide when you see clearly without the cloudiness of self-interest—when you are being. Sometimes this is a matter of time. When the time is right, the decision will become clear. If it doesn't seem clear, you must wait for the clouds and fog to leave. Always find out as much as you reasonably can before deciding.

Spencer in Hong Kong, ca. 1987

Don't Say Yes or No

Spencer and Kerstin
Tombstone, AZ, 2008

Always respond to inquiries, but be careful as to what you say. Honesty is one thing, stupidity is another. When in doubt – whenever that little red flag goes up or that uneasy feeling grips you—don't say yes and don't say no. Give yourself time to come to terms with whatever it is that has made you hesitate.

I used to have an employee who loved to catch me walking across the office grounds or cooking something in the employee lounge. She would shoot off these quick requests such as, "My staff has done such a great job on the blankety blank project, that I would love to take them out to lunch to celebrate. Is that OK?"

It would always sound simple and innocent enough on the face of it. But there would be some nagging aspect of it that I couldn't put my finger on immediately. She would hope for a quick yes without any thought being given to who would pay for the lunch (supposedly the company), who would fill in while her entire staff was gone, whether or not this was part of a budgeted item, whether or not her staff would be paid for the time spent at lunch, etc. On top of this, since we had a protocol for dealing with such requests, she was not following the standard procedure for authorization. To make matters worse, there were a few times when, caught off guard, I approved such things on the spot, thus encouraging this sort of behavior. Bad management. Bad judgment.

Don't say yes. Don't say no. In the above situation, the best response would be to throw the responsibility back to the employee: "Put it in writing, and I'll consider it." There are other responses to these sorts of requests for quick decisions. Phrases such as these below are pressure relief valves that can save you the agony of regret and the breaking of one of the five golden rules—Keep your agreements—because the odds are that if you jump into making quick decisions that you are not comfortable with, you will have to change your decision later on.

Here are some good responses:
- Let me think about that. I'll get back to you tomorrow (next week, etc.)
- I am going to think about it. We will discuss it at our meeting on Wednesday.
- I need more information before I can make a decision. Give me a complete analysis by Friday and we can discuss it on Monday.

By not committing to an instant decision, you truly give yourself time to consider the issues and ramifications of any decision you make. Sometimes this takes a little time. Also, notice that in many of these urgent situations, the urgency is created by the employee making the request, and the crisis is being placed onto your shoulders. Whenever possible, place the burden right back onto the back of the employee who created the problem in the first place.

Chapter 8
People

Are *these* the eyes of a Buffalo Exchange buyer?

Eyes that can discriminate between exciting style and drab rag. Eyes that work seven hours a day buying piece by piece the finest and most extensive inventory of recycled clothing in the city. Eyes that continuously weed out the mediocre from the excellent. Are these the eyes of a Buffalo Exchange buyer? Find out at either of our two shops.

NOW BUYING FALL CLOTHING

Shop at: **BUFFALO EXCHANGE**

The best of new and recycled clothing
Buying — Trading — Consigning

1072 N. Warren   22nd & Wilmot
795-6499   790-8350

Coping with Difficult People

Avoid them or get rid of them. We are all difficult at one time or another. Difficult people, however, are that way most of the time.

They take up a lot of time, suck energy from others, and disturb the workplace and the personal lives of those with whom they interact. First, you have to take time to deal with them, then you have to take time to deal with those who have dealt with them, then you have to take time to deal with the work that has been disrupted by dealing with them.

So why should we cope with them? Because coping with them when you can't get rid of them or avoid them is the best way of not having them be a destructive force and may, in fact, allow you to use the talents that they have. And very often, they do have useful talents.

As bosses, you are best advised to avoid hiring these folks. In that respect, what we will learn today may help you to do a better job in hiring.

Once hired and established in the work place, the laws and practicalities may make it impossible to do anything but deal with the situation.

If your boss or significant other or member of your social group is one of these, you are also going to be stuck with having to deal with these folks.

In any case, it is always better to have some coping strategies for dealing with difficult people rather than falling victim to their behavior.

Coping with difficult people is not easy and is not fun; but it can be rewarding if you manage to pull it off.

We cope with difficult people because we have to, don't deal with them if we don't have to. We fire them or break up with them or avoid spending time with them. They suck you dry, demoralize, make you feel bad, etc. If they can. But when you have to, you should have a handle on how to behave with them.

These are the five types of difficult people:

1. The Steamroller/The Bulldozer: This is what tends to work with these kinds of folks. Stand up to her/him, but don't fight. You won't win. Use her/his name. Tell her/him that you disagree, but ask her/him to explain their views further. Explain your position. If she/he interrupts you, stop her/him and tell them so. Don't sound angry or weak. Maintain eye contact on the same level.

2. The Complainer: Relax. Listen attentively. Listen actively. Interrupt once it becomes circular (if necessary). Keep to the point and respond with the facts. Engage her/him in the problem-solving; "What result would you like to see?" Ask for solutions and aim to win.

3. Clams: Silence is aggression. Wait and look invitingly expectant. Note the unresponsiveness and wait the same way again; if no success, apply positive pressure by suggesting that no response leaves you with little alternative.

4. Know-It-Alls: These are knowledgeable people. Do your homework and come with the facts. Feed back the main points that they make. Voice objections in the form of questions. Flow with their strengths. Subservience can go a long way with these folks.

5. Super-Agreeables: They are unreliable. They need to be liked, so assure them that they are OK and that you like them. Let them know that you want their honesty. Offer compromises before they do.

When in doubt, look to *The Wizard of Oz* and the Five Points of Power.

They may not work all of the time, but they are the basis for some good behavior habits that can at least save you in a pinch and are the basis for forming the truly meaningful relationships with normal people, if you happen to know any.

The Art of Throwing Darts in the Dark
Hiring is a Turkey Shoot

Being a poor manager, I had to hire 'em, fire 'em, and inspire 'em in between, although the "inspire 'em" part was on a pretty lean reinforcement level.

You have to hire people who can work with you and your style. My style was to expect that they could do the job if I showed them how. If they needed to be patted on the back every five minutes, I was the wrong manager for this person. If they were not smart, then they were the wrong employee for me, and if they didn't love doing a good job for its own sake, then we had nothing in common in the wonderful world of work. I also didn't want any weirdos around me. I was weird enough for me. Of course, it turned out those people I thought were normal were viewed by the rest of society as weird. Gays, nerds, religious fanatics, fashion-passion, tattooed, pierced, bad-hair people seemed perfectly OK to Kerstin and me. It was the ones that tried to ingratiate themselves to you, covered incompetence with lies—those sorts—that we could not abide.

Incompetence—whether based on native inability or a disoriented mental state—was the one thing that brought us to the firing squad.

Incompetence is the enemy of success. In business, it is the dark angel of death that you want to stay away from. When you come face to face with it, dispatch it. Get rid of it as soon as you can.

Get rid of incompetence as fast as you can. Work with a standardized progressive discipline plan, so that you document all problems and so that they can be shown to have been pondered in any way by any standard.

Hiring and the Art of Dog Selection

Most of this story is true; it happened about a month ago—a short enough time to avoid most of the memory loss, but long enough to allow for some embellishment.

The dog came in the night, we think, probably dumped just before giving birth to four or five pups. Out of 18 acres, she decided that right next to our garage under a bush and a tree was the best place to give birth. She then proceeded to defend her biological heritage in a most ferocious manner, making the 20 feet from the house to our cars very threatening.

The first night I saw her or the glimpses of her in the dark, it was raining and very cold. She looked like she might be a pit bull. She had to be wet; but it was hard to get close. I had fantasies of being bitten and then not being able to keep track of the dog, leading to rabies shots, which would not be the best thing for my compromised immune system. Imagine: dying of rabies instead of cancer. What irony. "What an imagination," you're thinking. Or, "What a nut case." But I digress.

The county animal control folks did not come to get rid of all this bother for four days, during which time, Kerstin, friend to all the creatures of the world, insisted on feeding the mother. When they did come, they were only able to capture the pups. The mother, they said, was much too wary and would have to be caught in a giant wire trap, which they baited alternately with special trapping food and their leftover McDonald's burgers. They strongly cautioned us against feeding her. They did not think she was a pit bull. They thought the pups would have a good chance at adoption and would be kept healthy by being given to a couple of lactating females that they had at their facility. "Great," I thought, "Come back soon and reunite the mother with her pups."

Never happened. After five days of us not feeding her and the only food available being in the big trap, we came home to a note that read: "She is too smart for us. We need the trap elsewhere."

Fast forward. Her name is Zillionaire—Zillie for short. Sixty two pounds on the vet's scale. She goes back to the vet on Monday for a little snipping here and there to prevent any more pups. When Kerstin drives up, Zillie whines in excitement. Pet her long enough and she flips over for a belly rub. She still lives outside, but in plush comfort. She'll walk on a leash without pulling. She will sit and stay, and, unlike so many dogs in this neighborhood, she does not bark at coyotes or other things in the dark. She barks only when something important is going on. The vet says she is between one and two years old. I think less than a year. She doesn't try to run off. Wherever we are, she is.

I would have never hired Zillie. First, I didn't want a dog at all. Second, I thought if I ever got a dog, it might weigh 20 pounds tops—something I could lift easily and pop in the car or keep under my desk at work. Also, I imagined a pooch that would smile. Zillie has a serious demeanor. Also, it would have to be a puppy, so it would bond with us and we would have total control over its upbringing to avoid any traumas or incorrect training or lack thereof as has been the case with all our other dogs in years past—the ones that chased rabbits into the desert all night and came back smelling like skunk, or chased cars wildly snapping at the rotating tires, etc.

No, I would have never hired Zillie. The experience has led me to think of all the people I have failed to hire, because they didn't have the right countenance, made a bad first impression, reminded me of a past problem employee, or were denied my approval for some other more repressed but nevertheless unjustifiable reason. I must have missed some—failed to hire that diamond and gotten to know and work with her or him. We always tout the successful hires and bemoan the failures; but we seldom look at the "pass pile."

I know that we now have hiring methods that are much more sophisticated. We have the drill-down interviewing methods, the Private Investigator, and background checking to help us with our selection process. Still, there is that subjective and therefore prejudiced aspect of any choosing that is deservedly an important part of the process; but a part that has to be continuously examined. The hidden criteria should be brought into consciousness—the light of day—to increase the possibilities of maybe going from a 20-pound to a 62-pound gem.

Spencer and Zillie

Basics of Hiring

Managing people is simple—not easy—but simple. Unless you set yourself up to function without any help, your greatest challenge in business will be the management of people. People who work with you can be your key to your success or failure. You have to learn to pick them, train them, educate them, and then manage them.

Your gut feelings about people are not without some merit. But everyone has blind areas. For some male managers, it's pretty young women. For some female managers, it's charming young men. Whatever your particular weak areas in judging people, you will generally do much better in the selection process if you base a large part of your choice making on past performance.

The best predictor of future performance is past performance. The best way to find out about past performance is to ask about it. Ask the candidate, ask his references and former employers, and pay close attention to what they all say or don't say!

In interviewing candidates, use a drill-down method that asks for specific incidents and specific behaviors and dialogs.

In short, use your gut only after you have done a complete and objective analysis and are having to decide between candidates who have measured up to your standards. Then, if all else is equal, pick the one you like the best.

After Finding Your Heart

Joseph Campbell said, "Follow Your Bliss." My dad said, "If you love your work, you are twice blessed: you get to eat and have a good time."

So, what happened after we found our true love: fashion? First, we took a good look at who we were hiring to work in our stores. Since everyone who worked in a store also bought, we immediately realized that the major criteria for hiring at the store level had to be fashion. This had not been the case for quite a while. We had allowed the concept of good customer service to become a major priority and lost our way. We spent much time and energy training for customer service and focused our hiring on "nice" people. Now, we began to focus on whether or not the individual had the eye and the passion. "Passion for Fashion" became the mantra.

Then we looked for the ability to relate to people. We had to turn down individuals who were not people friendly. This was a problem, because many fashion-passion people are cool, and cool means keeping your emotions to yourself. We needed people who wanted to develop emotional relations with our customers—our fellow lovers of this fine art. Loving clothing and people became major criteria for getting hired. We could and still do teach the rest.

Now the "eye" is an interesting phenomenon. What we found over the years was that not all fashion-loving people could necessarily see what to buy and certainly would not intuitively know how to price items when buying from the public. In addition, the "eye" involved not only seeing what was saleable and what was not, but it involved making an objective and impartial judgment about this, while relating on an emotional level with the seller. Not too many people could do this.

The "eye" involved seeing what would sell, not only what was aesthetically gratifying. It involved being able to objectify, to remember items and prices and labels, to understand clothing construction, to know materials, etc. Some of it we could train, but the basic talent had to be there along with the drive to make it happen.

Buffalo Exchange Staff, 1983

So You Want to Work Here

Share a vision and make it happen. Because the chances of success are greater working for a company whose values you share, we offer a glimpse of some of ours:

We believe what Buffalo Exchange does the recycling and re-using of fashion, contributes to making the world a better place.

We believe in hard work, integrity, respect for individuals and the necessity of individuals taking full responsibility for their actions and decisions.

Buffalo Exchange believes that work should be a joyous part of living, an extension of the person, and a path toward self-exploration and self-realization.

A love of fashion and clothing is essential. Buffalo Exchange is an equal opportunity employer. We consider all applicants for all positions without regard to race, color, religion, creed, gender, national origin, age, disability, marital or veteran status, or any other legally protected status.

I was thinking of adding this to the employment section of our company website:

- We believe that working for Buffalo Exchange is not for everyone.

- We are a well-structured company that is continously evolving and finding our way through the maze of wonders and challenges that make up the world of business.

- We ask of our employees that they participate in learning about business and enter with us into this adventure.

- Those who just want a job seldom do well in our environment.

A Note to Serious Applicants

Buffalo Exchange is a family-owned company. As such, it is run with certain peculiarities and idiosyncrasies. Our screening procedures for applicants are specific to us and to the position. We are an equal opportunity employer. However, we do discriminate against dishonesty, haughtiness, inefficiency, inability to listen, lack of personal integrity and fortitude, etc.

You get the idea.

In addition to all the above, the position will require that you bring to it both the strength and intelligence needed to manage high-level people as well as the humility to integrate your management style with ours. It is going to be a tough job.

We like tough—tough love, tough work. We like fun. We believe that the two co-exist easily in our environment.

Be aware that one of our great abilities as an organization lies in cutting through camouflage, deceit, and obfuscation.

Company meeting at Disneyland, 2007

Get the Right Person in the Right Spot

The Unification Theory of Management is simple. It's all made up of people, nothing else.

People are all that count. Selecting people is the most important function of the job.

- If you get the right person in the right spot, success is easy.
- If you get a person in the wrong spot, failure is guaranteed.

It's the individual—only the individual. This is the basic building block.

It's not the structure. Structure does not matter. Only the individual matters.

If the individual is superior, structure will follow or will not be needed at all. Quality people are worth whatever you pay them.

Vella Austin, 1979

Chapter 9
and in the end...

A Short Cancer Tale

Spencer and Tito at the Mayo Clinic, 2005

In April 2005, I was diagnosed with pancreatic cancer. In order to be operable, the tumor had to be reduced in size. For six weeks, I lived part time in Scottsdale, Arizona, undergoing a simultaneous treatment of radiation and chemotherapy, which was successful in shrinking the tumor.

On September 29th, I had surgery to remove the tumor and restructure and/or remove some of my internal organs. After 11 fairly bad days in the Mayo Clinic Hospital, I came home weak and skinny for an eight week recuperation period.

I made it back to health and now begin what I hope will be the last round of chemotherapy, which I will do here in Tucson. This is what I refer to as the "insurance policy."

Many people are lucky in marriage—another, miracle of life. I am fortunate to be one of these. I am not sure if I would be here now if it were not for my love. To try to explain any more seems feeble. I stand in awe of what she did for me.

That has been my year. I have been too turned in toward myself and my survival; but it has made me much more aware of the troubles and struggles of others. I have listened patiently and with great empathy to a son tell me of his father suffering from cancer and choosing to stop his chemo treatment and die rather than continue to be ravaged by the side effects of the treatment.

I understood in the deepest part of me what that was about. I wept when I heard of the father's death.

And, oh, I have wept more this year than in the previous decade for everything from dying dogs in New Orleans to dying fictional characters in movies and books.

This has been my year. I will have many more, but will always remember this one and hopefully the lessons I had to learn.

> Of all the money e'er I had,
> I spent it in good company.
> And all the harm I've ever done,
> Alas! It was to none but me.
> And all I've done for want of wit
> To mem'ry now I can't recall
> So fill to me the parting glass
> Good night and joy be with you all*

I will sing this little Irish diddy with some re-wording:

> Of all the workin' time I spent
> I've done it in good company
> And all the harm that ever I did
> Alas it was to none but me
> And all I did for want of wit
> To memory I cannot recall
> So fill to me the wishin' glass
> Good health and job be with you all

* The Parting Glass is a traditional Irish song, often sung at the end of a gathering with friends.

My Year in Review - By Spencer

This was the year of my 65th birthday. It was a year of enriched friendships and hard living. It was a year of great indebtedness. It was a year of great insights at many levels—spiritual, philosophical, and emotional.

Yet, as the year comes to a close and I feel mostly healed from my battle with cancer, I find myself again driving my car in the fast lane and zipping in and out of traffic. Although it's just a little bit of time, it still amazes me that I do it at all. Have I learned nothing?

After the Tooth Fairy, and Santa, for so many of us, there is nothing left to believe in. The true magic, the true fairy tale of all time—life—is but an everyday part of our existence that we pass over just as we swat at a fly on a lazy summer day.

There's about 50 years between the Tooth Fairy and an understanding of the miracle of life. For some people, of course, there is not time, since the vacuum after the Tooth Fairy envelopes them for all of their lives.

What other great things happened this year? I got to go on two trips on the boat, the Buffalo Gal II. Our cabin got finished, and we have gotten to spend more time on Mt. Lemmon.

Spencer on the Buffalo Gal II, 2006

Remember: Business is a Form of War

Remember, business is a form of war. Those who hate war, even non-deadly war, should work for someone else.

Peace is war in disguise.

Today I am on steroids. I had a chemotherapy treatment yesterday, and they give you steroids to help your body handle the poison. By tomorrow afternoon, I will become very tired and will go home early. Thursday, I will stay home. Friday I will be back here for our 10:00 a.m. Board meeting. The Board consists of Kerstin, Rebecca, and me.

Cancer has some benefits that most people don't seem to realize:

- When you hear a bird sing, it sounds a lot more magnificent than before.
- Flowers look different.
- In short, the world seems much brighter and clearer.
- My work here has become much better focused.
- Also, you tend not to mince your words. There's no point in it. You speak a little more directly.

Spencer, 2006

Engaging the World

I love these hard times. I love the scary part. I love the idea that Buffalo Exchange may be in danger. I relish the simplicity of fear and opportunity, the shedding of the complexities that obfuscate the obvious and have allowed us all to diminish the value of work, the true precious value of a job. And I have been angered by my own seduction into believing that the jobs that we offer the world do not have the worth that they truly do have. It has taken this economic shake to jerk me out of my complacency.

I have a friend who feels that every day he works is a day of lost time. What a sad and dismal view that is. Work is what life is. Work is a glorious extension of who you are and probably the most exciting opportunity to engage in the world. Work done well is a joy and a great fulfillment. It's nice to get a big salary. Hell, it's good to be King. But to have work to do is the thing. If you can do what you enjoy and are good at and still put food on the table and a roof over your head, you are truly blessed. To lust after money and power and be forever unsatisfied is a curse. And I know of no one who chases money and is ever satisfied.

Bryce Fitzgerald died April 19, 2009. His cancer came and took him quickly. Friends he had made here at the General Administration office in Tucson were incredibly supportive of him in his final months. I stand in awe of their commitment and show of compassion and nurturing.

Bryce worked here almost a decade, driving and getting things, implanting his being among us. He liked the job and did it well. There was great affection between Bryce and his fellow workers. When he retired, he stayed very busy and seemed to enjoy his leisure time.

When someone passes on, what's left is the memory. We all will have different memories.

I remember a humble, kind, sensitive, thoughtful, good man who liked his work and took sustenance from it. As long as there are those of us who remember, Bryce lives on.

Kerstin, Bryce, and Spencer, 2005

Interview with Myself

Philosophy of Life?

There is nothing but life. God is life. I wish it were otherwise, but I have not been so blessed. The whole of life is made up of small decisions and small miracles like a maze of stepping stones across a great river. The trick is not to fall in. But one way or another, we all make it to the other side; which ironically turns out to be just like the side we left. The joy is in the crossing.

Who is your favorite poet?

Now, even more, I appreciate those couplets from Robert Frost:

> *"Forgive, O Lord, my little jokes on thee,*
> *And I will forgive Thy great big one on me"*
> In the Clearing, 1962

> *"The old dog barks backwards*
> *Without getting up*
> *I can remember when he was a pup"*
> The Span of Life, 1936

Since I read very little, Frost is my favorite.

What is your favorite music?

It changes to some extent; but the enduring preferences are classical, some jazz, Frank Sinatra, Irish, Bluegrass (without the whiny voices), mostly instrumental music.

Who is your favorite person?

My children and grandchildren and of all my wife, who is miraculous in so many ways that I would list, except that this is my interview, and who, for whatever reason that I don't understand, accepts me for what I am and allows me the freedom to be that.

Would you say you are self-absorbed?

Jesus! Doesn't this interview prove it! I have had to come to terms with being a little man with no extraordinary talent or skills. I would say that my accomplishments have been relatively minor with the possible exception of Buffalo Exchange, which owes its early expansion to my basic discontent with the state of things in general and a pretty good sense for the retail business and people. I stay happy despite this understanding that our entire civilization and I are but microscopic specks in the universe. But I would still like to have been famous.

What is your greatest strength?

Problem solving. Being relegated to a life outside the "box." By virtue of a poor memory, a restless mind, and difficulty in thinking in straight lines, I often see solutions that others do not. However, this must be seen in the context of one who would like to be in the "box," which is a permanent condition of one having my personality characteristics.

What is your greatest weakness?

All of the above combined with a great need to be liked, combined with a great dislike of this need.

What is your favorite food?

Anything that tastes good, can be digested easily by the enzymes I take, does not spike my insulin production, and does not introduce nasty chemicals into my body. Oh, and it should not raise my cholesterol count. That pretty well narrows it down to a very few foods and since having most of my pancreas gone leaves my tastes changing fairly dramatically from time to time, the list of possible foods is ever changing and limited.

Spencer, 2006

The Way of the Buffalo
(2009)

For thousands of years, bison roamed North America in massive herds, ranging from the Great Slave Lake in Canada's far north to Mexico in the south, and from eastern Oregon almost to the Atlantic Ocean. These herds trampled the earth, grazing the land down to the last niblets of green, then fertilizing, trampling more, and moving on, leaving the earth enriched and turned and ready to spring back in an eternal cycle of natural rejuvenation. These giants of the prairies survived in gentle blissful harmony with the land they inhabited. That was the buffalo way.

By a quirk of fate, we named our company after these glorious animals; and without conscious intent, took on one of their sterling traits: the integrative and mutually beneficial relationship to our surrounding. We added our sense of morality and balance, our ability to deal with human beings, our understanding of business, and this became our buffalo way.

The North American bison population was decimated through greed, ignorance, and the cruel goal of genocide. Only recently we have stood witness to the decimation of our economic system, victimized by many of the same excesses, the same human weakness. The buffalo stands today both as a symbol of the worst of a culture and as a memory of what glory there was when humans were in balance with the natural order of the earth. As a company bearing this symbol, whether by initial intent or not, we have come to accept it as our reminder of what happens when a culture or a company has only the limited goal of profit at any cost.

Our goal throughout these 35 years has always been first and foremost to make a profit, to earn a living, to be able to pay our bills and put food on the table; but always to do it with honesty and integrity. In those instances where we have failed to live up to our own standards of decency and righteousness, or where we have made bad decisions about business and/or people, we have been able to step outside of ourselves, look at ourselves, acknowledge our faults, make amends as best we can, and do better.

We have asked this of all who work for us. We have gotten better, all of us, better at who we are and at what we do.

When Woody Allen was asked what he thought the most important element in any successful relationship was, he responded with one word: "luck."

I was fortunate enough to have married a person that I could live with and who could live with me. We entered business together and never doubted each other, even when we didn't know where we were going or how to get there. We were compatible. We complimented each other. We were able to grow together in directions that allowed us to be together and still explore our own ways. I stayed out of her way and she out of mine, at least most of the time. Whatever small differences we have had, we have had a common belief concerning business. We both believed that Buffalo Exchange was an educational organization, a training place for those willing to continuously grow and learn.

From the beginning, both Kerstin and I believed in having fun. We believed that there should be great joy in working, that there should be excitement, adventure, exploration, challenge, and enjoyment in work. If there was no laughter, there wasn't much point in doing it. We had both had jobs that brought us money but no real enjoyment. That seemed OK for the short haul. But for the marathon—for the 35 year run—the 100-year run—enjoyment had to be built into the life of the company.

I have been doubly blessed to be in a partnership with a couple of business wizards. In the last 19 years, Rebecca has taken on the job of managing a large portion of Buffalo Exchange and has done it with fervor and competency that has amazed me. Much of our growth has occurred during this time, and it's no coincidence. Her common sense, her quick grasp of complex issues, her knowledge of the industry, her fashion sense, and her ability to work with all sorts of people, including me, has made her a great force in the building of our company.

We have been fortunate that we deal with something as joyous as fashion and as wacky, amazing, and challenging as people. It's a wonderful combination that has made these 35 years a true blessing.

Spencer, Rebecca, and Kerstin Block
Buffalo Exchange 35th Anniversary Party

Exit Strategy

So, nobody has asked me what my exit strategy is except, of course, my lawyer and my accountant. Do you all know what an exit strategy is? It's how you extricate yourself from a business that you have built up. Some exit strategies involve selling the company, taking the company public, walking away and letting the company fade into oblivion—you get the idea. It's that well deserved retirement that I keep hearing about.

Well, after years of hard thinking, I finally realized what my exit strategy was. I finally figured it out. I share it with you now, since you all seem to be sitting on the edge of your seats. MY EXIT STRATEGY IS DEATH. It's the only logical conclusion I could come to. I'll quit when I don't need food and shelter any more.

Spencer, National Association of
Resale & Thrift Stores conference, 2009

In Memory of Spencer Block

March 27, 1940 - September 6, 2009
Obituary

Spencer Block loved life. He loved his wife and his family. He loved his friends, his employees, and his business. He loved boating, music, and computers. He did not want to leave this life. After four and a half years of living with pancreatic cancer, his body finally had enough. He passed away at his home, as he wished, peacefully, with his family around him.

Spencer was a teacher, a librarian, a counselor, and, finally, a business owner.

With his wife he started Buffalo Exchange 35 years ago. He worked there until his death.

He is missed by his wife of 47 years, Kerstin; his daughters, Rebecca (Tim Haskin) and Karen; his three granddaughters, his brother, and his many friends and co-workers.

There is a part of him that will live on in all of us; if we think on it, we all know what "Spencer would say and do."

His ability to be fair, look at all sides of a situation, and speak the truth were hallmarks of his approach to life.

There will be no services. His ashes will be distributed per his wishes. A commemorative gathering for family and friends will take place this fall.

Spencer Block:
Scant Fashion Sense, Tons of Business Savvy
By Kimberly Matas, Arizona Daily Star

September 10, 2009

Spencer Block was never much of a fashionista.

He had a rotation of jeans, Hawaiian shirts and blue Oxfords in his closet and seldom strayed from his comfortable, casual wardrobe.

One would never know that the former elementary school teacher, librarian and son of a Chicago fish monger was co-founder of multimillion-dollar Tucson-based national clothing chain Buffalo Exchange.

"He was banned from the buying room," said his wife, Kerstin. "He was not a fashion-interested person. I shopped for him," usually from the racks of their own stores.

Block's business savvy, combined with his wife's fashion sense, built a used-clothing empire from their original store, a tiny retail space they opened near the University of Arizona in 1974.

It's a testament to Block's acumen in retail that the team of employees and business associates he mentored over the years will be able to run the company in his absence. Block died at home Sunday, the result of a 4 1/2-year struggle with pancreatic cancer. He was 69. A memorial for family and friends will be scheduled in the autumn.

Block learned about business from his father. As a boy, he got hands-on experience working in the family fish market. Later, he worked behind the scenes as the accountant.

Block was an English major at the University of Arizona

in 1960 when he met his future bride on campus. Kerstin was a Swedish anthropology student studying abroad for a year. When she went back to Sweden, Block followed. Eventually the couple returned to the States and Block's hometown of Chicago, where he earned a bachelor's degree in education and taught elementary school. From Illinois, the couple moved to Oregon, where Block continued teaching while earning a master's in psychology.

A job at a Bureau of Indian Affairs boarding school in Fort Apache brought the Blocks back to Arizona. After a year, they moved to Tucson, and Spencer returned to the UA for a second master's, this one in library science. It was while he was working as a librarian that his wife got the idea to open a clothing store that bought, sold and traded merchandise. Kerstin wanted a thoroughly American name for the store, and the buffalo was an iconic symbol of her adopted country. The word "exchange" simply described what they did.

Kerstin was the public face of the company while her husband preferred working behind the scenes.

"We had different talents, and it was a fortunate thing," said his wife of 47 years. "We were able to combine our talents to work together and create this company."

Greg Furrier, a partner in Picor Commercial Real Estate Services, had worked with Spencer over the years on property deals and was impressed with Block's astute business sense.

"They had a really good business model," Furrier said. "What really surprises people in Tucson is that the company is much bigger than anyone realizes."

Since opening their first small shop 35 years ago, Buffalo Exchange has grown to nearly 40 stores in a dozen states with annual sales totaling $56.3 million. Their company has been mentioned on television — "Good Morning America," CNN, "Today" — and in national magazines, including *Time, Forbes, Elle* and *Vogue*.

"They always bought cutting-edge kinds of fashions and they were really tuned into their customers," Furrier said.

Even with all their success, the couple, along with one of their daughters, Rebecca Block, continued to oversee operation of their Tucson stores. The Blocks' other daughter, Karen Bailey, also lives in Tucson. Chief Operations Officer Vella Austin has been with Buffalo Exchange for 30 years. She worked her way up from her first position, as manager of the Tempe store.

"I learned everything about doing this job, and business in general, from Spencer Block," she said. "I think he operated quite a bit from his gut. He had his own philosophy he created Buffalo Exchange from. A lot of it had to do with being fair and honest.

"He means the world to me. I'm going to miss seeing Spencer in his Hawaiian shirts. He had one on every day."

As their company grew, the Blocks shared their success. Patrons of the arts, they awarded up to $10,000 annually to a local artist. Last year, the company was lauded at the Better Business Bureau of Southern Arizona's annual ethics awards for its Tokens for Bags program that has generated more than $265,000 in donations to hundreds of nonprofit groups since 1994. They've supported Tucson charities for medical research, families in need and homeless teens. And they've given generously to local political campaigns.

"We realized early on that we wanted to give back to the community as much as we could," Kerstin Block said.

Her husband was equally magnanimous with his time, serving on community boards and government committees to benefit small-business owners and Pima County residents.

Block was a prolific writer of letters to the editor, and his concerns ran the gamut from global warming, gay marriage and human rights to energy conservation, environmental protection and the death of Fred Rogers, host of the PBS show "Mister Rogers' Neighborhood."

Though Block described himself and his wife as "people of the '60s," in a 2004 Arizona Daily Star article, he also was a socially responsible capitalist. It says as much on the company website.

It's a philosophy Block crafted for his company and for his life and hinges on integrity, personal responsibility and having fun.

"There are lots of different ways that companies can branch out," Spencer Block said in 2004. "If they get too big, they can lose their soul. We have a nice spirit about it."

Kerstin and Rebecca at the All Souls Procession, 2009

Hawaiians Die

Hawaiians die
Sitting under coconut trees
In the peace of an ocean breeze
All the same they die
Just like you and I

Spencer in Hawaii, 2001

"We are stuck to and with each other, and this is
where life takes place.
Every interaction is a replay
of the most primitive social act—communicating,
keeping each other company."

—Spencer Block

Photo descriptions:

Page vii: Buffalo Exchange company meeting held in November 2009 in San Diego, California; present are all store and General Administration management.

Page 14: Exterior view of the first Buffalo Exchange store at 1070 N. Warren, Tucson, Arizona; opened January 15, 1974.

Page 16: Spencer and Kerstin Block inside the 1070 N. Warren store, ca. 1975.

Chapter 1: Spencer in an early ad for Buffalo Exchange, 1979.

Page 19: A greeting card from Yellowstone National Park.

Page 20: Buffalo Exchange logo created for the 2009, 35th anniversary of the company.

Page 21: Spencer posing for a photo shoot to be used in an ad campaign for Buffalo Exchange, ca. 1975.

Page 23: Kerstin Block and Ruth Williams, a long-time customer of Buffalo Exchange, ca. 1995.

Page 28: Kerstin Block and their cat, Ira, ca. 1978.

Chapter 2: Buffalo Exchange ad, 1974.

Page 36: Mark Weiss, family friend, guru, and business consultant.

Page 39: Canoe Pickett, Spencer and Kerstin Block during a photoshoot for Buffalo Exchange, 1994.

Page 42: Spencer Block, ca. 1980.

Page 45: Kerstin, Karen, Rebecca Block with staff and friends during a photoshoot for Buffalo Exchange. Taken at 1070 N. Warren in 1974.

Chapter 3: Ad for Buffalo Exchange, ca. 1980.

Page 52: Spencer and Kerstin at the 2001 E. Speedway store, for the 30th anniversary party of Buffalo Exchange, 2004.

Page 53: Spencer Block's grandmother; he referred to her as Buby Rose, Buby being Yiddish for grandmother. Taken in Tucson, Arizona, ca. 1960.

Page 55: Spencer and his parents; Milton and Dorothy Block, ca. 1980.

Page 57: Buffalo Exchange company meeting, celebrating the 20th anniversary, 1994.
Page 59: Spencer Block, 2006.

Chapter 4: Buffalo Exchange 2004 Christmas card.
Page 64: Buffalo Exchange's annual Halloween pumpkin carving contest, 2004. Replica of the trailer used during Spencer and Kerstin's 30th anniversary tour of the stores.
Page 65: McKenzie Harrison, modeling for a Buffalo Exchange photo shoot in 2000.
Page 66: Kerstin and Zillie walking in the desert near their home, ca. 2008.
Page 67: Spencer and Kerstin, December 2007.
Page 69: The X Team in Mexico, 2000. Todd Colletti, Michelle Livingston, Rebecca Block, David Ziegler-Voll, Dana Whitney, Spencer Block, Sabrina Barger, and Francis Peterson.

Chapter 5: Earth Day celebration flyer for Buffalo Exchange stores Dollar Day event, 2008, sponsoring the Galapagos Conservancy.
Page 75: Spencer Block, 1950, age 10.
Page 77: Buffalo Exchange Arts Award plaque, designed by Janet K. Miller, 2010.
Page 79: Buffalo Exchange "Tokens for Bag" token, given to customers instead of a bag. Each token received gives $.05 to a charity chosen by the store.

Chapter 6: Spencer Block in a Buffalo Exchange ad, ca. 1978.
Page 84: Spencer Block and Vella Austin, 1996. Vella is the Buffalo Exchange Chief Operations Officer and has been an employee of the company since 1979.
Page 88: Tito Haggardt and Spencer Block in Tucson, Arizona, in 2000. Tito is a long-time family friend.
Page 89: Spencer and his granddaughter, Melissa Haskin, playing on a stone seal sculpture at Friday Harbor, San Juan Islands, Washington, 2005.
Page 90: Spencer Block on his boat the Buffalo Gal II, ca. 2000.

Page 91: Spencer and Kerstin Block in Kona,Hawaii, posing with tropical birds, ca. 1996.

Page 93: Spencer Block dressed in a Indian Hindu costume at the Buffalo Exchange Halloween party, 2004.

Page 95: Spencer Block, 1997, at Mt. Lemmon, preparing to play in the Mt. Lemmon Marching Mandolin Band, which Spencer founded.

Chapter 7: Buffalo Exchange ad, ca. 1995. The bowling shirt was given to Spencer by Todd Colletti, Colorado franchise owner.

Page 100: Spencer in his home office, 2008.

Page 103: Buffalo Exchange ad used in the fall of 2000.

Page 106: Milton Block in front of his company truck, taken in Chicago, Illinois, ca. 1980.

Page 107: Kerstin and Spencer Block, photo taken January 2009, at the Buffalo Exchange End of the Year Awards Dinner; the theme was vintage country western.

Page 109: Spencer dressed as the Emperor of China, taken in Hong Kong, ca. 1987.

Page 110: Spencer, Kerstin, and Zillie in Tombstone, Arizona, 2008.

Chapter 8: Buffalo Exchange ad, ca. 1979.

Page 120: Spencer and Zillie at their home, 2008.

Page 123: Buffalo Exchange staff during a photo shoot in 1983, posing in 1950s attire in front of the 803 E. Helen store in Tucson, Arizona.

Page 125: Spencer in Disneyland, during the Buffalo Exchange company meeting in 2007.

Page 126: Vella Austin at the Tempe, Arizona store in 1979.

Chapter 9: Buffalo Exchange ad, 2008-2009.

Page 129: Spencer and Tito Haggardt at the Mayo Clinic in Phoenix, Arizona, 2005.

Page 131: Spencer on his boat, the Buffalo Gal II, 2006.

Page 132: Spencer in 2006.